Judaism Today

Continuum *Religion Today*

These useful guides aim to introduce religions through the lens of contemporary issues, illustrated throughout with examples and case studies taken from lived religion. The perfect companion for the student of religion, each guide interprets the teachings of the religion in question in a modern context and applies them to modern-day scenarios.

Forthcoming:
Christianity Today, George D. Chryssides
Hinduism Today, Stephen Jacobs
Islam Today, Ron Geaves
Sikhism Today, Jagbir Jhutti-Johal

Judaism Today

Dan Cohn-Sherbok

continuum

Continuum International Publishing Group

The Tower Building
11 York Road
London SE1 7NX

80 Maiden Lane
Suite 704
New York NY 10038

www.continuumbooks.com

British Library Cataloguing-in-Publication Data
A catalogue record for this book is available from the British Library.

ISBN: HB: 978-0-8264-3829-4
         PB: 978-0-8264-2231-6

Library of Congress Cataloging-in-Publication Data
Cohn-Sherbok, Dan.
  Judaism today / Dan Cohn-Sherbok.
     p. cm.
  Includes index.
  ISBN 978-0-8264-3829-4 — ISBN 978-0-8264-2231-6 1. Judaism—History—Modern period, 1750- 2. Jewish sects—History—19th century. 3. Jewish sects—History—20th century. I. Title.
  BM195.C636 2010
  296.09'051—dc22
                          2009045430

Typeset by Free Range Book Design & Production
Printed and bound in Great Britain by CPI Antony Rowe Ltd, Chippenham, Wiltshire

Contents

For Lavinia

Preface

For nearly four millennia Judaism was an essentially monolithic system based on shared traditions. Despite the emergence of various subgroups through the centuries such as the Sadducees, Pharisees, Essenes, Karaites, Shabbateans and Hasidim, Jewry was united in the belief in a providential God who had chosen the Jews as his special people and given them a code of law. In the modern period, however, the Jewish religion has fragmented into a series of separate denominations with competing ideologies and theological views. Despite the creation of the State of Israel, the Jewish people are deeply divided concerning the most fundamental issues of belief and practice. Most textbooks have focused on the historical or theological aspects of the Jewish faith as it developed over the centuries. Unlike these introductions to Judaism, this guide explores Judaism as it is actually practised today and takes onboard the issues debated amongst Jews that will shape its future. There is an additional Companion Website accompanying this book – details are given on the back cover.

Introduction

The Historical Background

Jews in the Ancient World

The history of the Jewish people began in Mesopotamia, where successive empires of the ancient world flourished and decayed before the Jews emerged as a separate people. The culture of these civilizations had a profound impact on the Jewish religion – ancient Near Eastern myths were refashioned to serve the needs of the Hebrew people. It appears that the Jews emerged in this milieu as a separate nation between the nineteenth and sixteenth centuries BCE. According to the Bible, Abraham was the father of the Jewish people. Initially known as Abram, he came from Ur of the Chaldeans. Together with his family he went to Haran and subsequently to Canaan, later settling in the plain near Hebron. Abraham was followed by Isaac and Jacob, who came to be known as Israel. Eventually Jacob's son Joseph was sold into slavery in Egypt. There he prospered, becoming a vizier in the house of Pharaoh. In time, the entire Hebrew clan moved to Egypt, where they remained and flourished for centuries until a new Pharaoh decreed that all first-born Hebrews should be put to death.

Jacob Wrestling with the Angel

The Book of Genesis describes Jacob's encounter at Peniel, where his name was changed to Israel:

> When the messenger of God saw that he did not prevail against Jacob, he touched the hollow of his thigh; and Jacob's thigh was put out of joint as he wrestled with him. Then he said, 'Let me

go, for the day is breaking.' But Jacob said, 'I will not let you go, unless you bless me.' And he said to him, 'What is your name?' And he said, 'Your name shall no more be called Jacob, but Israel, for you have striven with God and with men and have prevailed.' (Genesis 32:25–8).

To persuade Pharaoh to let the Jewish people go, God sent a series of plagues upon the Egyptians. Following this devastation, Moses, the leader of the people, led his kinsfolk out of Egypt, and after wandering in the desert for forty years, the Hebrews finally entered into the land that God had promised them. Under Joshua's leadership, the Hebrews conquered the existing inhabitants, and after his death they started to form themselves into separate groups. At first there were 12 tribes named after the sons of Jacob: Joseph, Benjamin, Levi, Simeon, Reuben, Judah, Issachar, Zebulun, Dan, Naphtali, Gad and Asher. When Levi became a special priestly group excluded from this territorial division, the tribe of Joseph was divided into two and named after his sons: Ephraim and Manasseh. During this period the Hebrews were ruled over by 12 national heroes who served successively as judges.

Frequently the covenant between God and his chosen people – first formulated by Moses – was proclaimed at communal gatherings. Such an emphasis on covenantal obligation reinforced the belief that the Jews were the recipients of God's loving kindness. With the people now in a more settled existence, the covenant expanded to include additional legislation, including the provisions needed for an agricultural community. During this period it became increasingly clear to the Jewish nation that the God of the covenant directed human history: the Exodus and the entry into the Promised Land were viewed as the unfolding of a divine plan.

Mount Sinai

For the ancient Israelites, the revelation on Mount Sinai served as the basis of legal obligations:

On the morning of the third day there were thunders and light-nings, and a thick cloud upon the mountain, and a very loud trumpet blast, so that all the people who were in the camp trembled. Then Moses brought the people out of the camp to meet God; and they took their stand at the foot of the mountain.

And Mount Sinai was wrapped in smoke, because the Lord descended upon it in fire; and the smoke of it went up like the smoke of a kiln, and the whole mountain trembled greatly. And as the sound of the trumpet grew louder and louder, Moses spoke, and God answered him in thunder. And the Lord came down upon Mount Sinai, to the top of the mountain, and Moses went up. And the Lord said to Moses, 'Go down and warn the people, lest they break through to the Lord to gaze and many of them perish. And also let the priests who come near to the Lord consecrate themselves, lest the Lord break out upon them.' And Moses said to the Lord, 'The people cannot come up to Mount Sinai; for thou thyself didst charge us saying, "Set bounds about the mountain, and consecrate it."' And the Lord said to him, 'Go down, and come up bringing Aaron with you; but do not let the priests and the people break through to come up to the Lord, lest He break out against them.' So Moses went down to the people and told them. (Exodus 19:16–25)

Under the judges, God was conceived as the supreme monarch. When some tribes suggested to Gideon that he deserved a formal position of power, he declared that it was impossible for the nation to be ruled over by both God and a human king. Nonetheless, Saul was subsequently elected as king despite the prophet Samuel's warnings against the dangers of usurping God's rule. In later years the Israelite nation divided into two kingdoms. The northern tribes had been united only by their allegiance to King David. But when his successor King Solomon and his son Rehoboam violated many of the ancient traditions, the northern tribes revolted. Ostensibly this was a rebellion against the injustice of the monarchy, but in reality it was an attempt to recapture the simple faith of the generation that had escaped from Egypt. What the north looked for was allegiance and loyalty to the King of kings who had brought them back from Egyptian bondage into the Promised Land. It was against this background that the pre-exilic prophets endeavoured to bring the nation back to the true worship of God. During the first millennium BCE the Jews watched their country emerge as a powerful state, only to see it sink into spiritual and moral decay. Following the Babylonian conquest in 586 BCE the Temple lay in ruins, Jerusalem was demolished and they despaired of their fate. This was God's punishment for their iniquity, which the prophets had predicted. Yet despite defeat and exile, the nation rose from the ashes of the old kingdoms. In the centuries which followed, the

Jewish people continued their religious traditions and communal life. Though they had lost their independence, their devotion to God and his law sustained them through suffering and hardship and inspired them to new heights of creativity. In Babylonia the exiles flourished, keeping their religion alive in the synagogues. These institutions were founded so that Jews could meet together for worship and study; no sacrifices were offered since that was the prerogative of the Jerusalem Temple. When in 538 BCE King Cyrus of Persia permitted the Jews to return to their former home, the nation underwent a transformation. The Temple was rebuilt and religious reforms were enacted. This return to the land of their fathers led to national restoration and a renaissance of Jewish life that was to last until the first century CE.

The period following the death of King Herod in 4 BCE was a time of intense anti-Roman feeling among the Jewish population in Judea as well as in the diaspora. Eventually such hostility led to war, only to be followed by defeat and the destruction of the Jerusalem Temple. In 70 CE, thousands of Jews were deported. Such devastation, however, did not quell the Jewish hope of ridding the Holy Land of its Roman oppressors. In the second century a messianic rebellion led by Simeon Bar Kochba was crushed by Roman forces, which killed multitudes of Jews and decimated Judea. Yet despite this defeat, the Pharisees carried on the Jewish tradition through teaching and study at Javneh, near Jerusalem.

Rabbinic Judaism

From the first century BCE Palestinian rabbinic scholars engaged in the interpretation of Scripture. The most important scholar of the early rabbinic period was Judah ha-Nasi, the head of the Sanhedrin, whose main achievement was the redaction of the Mishnah in the second century CE. This volume consisted of the discussions and rulings of sages whose teachings had been transmitted orally. According to the rabbis, the law recorded in the Mishnah was given orally to Moses along with the written law: 'Moses received the Torah from Sinai, and handed it down to Joshua, and Joshua to the elders, and the elders to the prophets to the men of the Great Assembly.' This view recorded in the Mishnah implies that there was an infallible chain of transmission from Moses to the leaders of the nation and eventually to the Pharisees.

Jewish Learning in Palestine

Despite the loss of the Temple, the great Pharisaic tradition of learning and interpretation was preserved in the academy of Yavneh. Simon the Righteous used to say: 'The world stands on three things – on the Torah, on the Temple service, and on acts of kindness.' But his successor, Rabbi Simeon, son of Gamaliel, said: 'The world stands upon three things: upon justice, upon truth and upon peace.'[1]

The Sanhedrin, which had been so fundamental in the compilation of the Mishnah, met in several cities in Galilee, but later settled in the Roman district of Tiberius. Simultaneously, others scholars established their own schools in other parts of the country, where they applied the Mishnah to everyday life, together with old rabbinic teachings that had not been incorporated into the Mishnah. During the third century the Roman Empire encountered numerous difficulties, including inflation, population decline and a lack of technological development to support the army. In addition, rival generals struggled against one another for power, and the government became increasingly inefficient. Throughout this time of upheaval, the Jewish community underwent a similar decline as a result of famine, epidemics and plunder.

At the end of the third century the emperor Diocletian inaugurated reforms that strengthened the empire. In addition, Diocletian introduced measures to repress the spread of Christianity, which now presented a serious challenge to the official religion of the empire. But Diocletian's successor, Constantine the Great, reversed his predecessor's hostile stance and extended official toleration to Christians. By this stage Christianity had succeeded in gaining a substantial number of adherents among the urban population; eventually, Constantine became more involved in church affairs and, just before his death, he himself was baptized. The Christianization of the empire continued throughout the century, and by the early 400s Christianity was fully established as the state religion.

By the first half of the fourth century Jewish scholars in Israel had collected together the teachings of generations of rabbis in the academies of Tiberius, Caesarea and Sepphoris. These extended discussions of the Mishnah became the Palestinian Talmud. The views of these Palestinian teachers had an important influence on scholars in Babylonia, though this work never attained the same prominence as that of the Babylonian Talmud.

Paralleling the development of rabbinic Judaism in Palestine, Babylonian scholars founded centres of learning. The great third-century teacher Rav established an academy at Sura in central Mesopotamia; his contemporary Samuel was head of another Babylonian academy at Nehardea. After Nehardea was destroyed in an invasion in 259 CE, the school at Pumbeditha also became a dominant Babylonian academy of Jewish learning. The Babylonian sages carried on and developed the Galilean tradition of disputation, and the fourth century produced two of the most distinguished scholars of the talmudic period, Abbaye and Rava, who both taught at Pumbeditha. With the decline of Jewish institutions in Israel, Babylonia became the most important centre of Jewish scholarship.

By the sixth century Babylonian scholars completed the redaction of the Babylonian Talmud, an editorial task begun by Rav Ashi in the fourth to fifth century at Sura. This major work parallels the Palestinian Talmud and is largely a summary of the rabbinic discussions that took place in the Babylonian academies. Both Talmuds are essentially elaborations of the Mishnah. The text itself consists largely of summaries of rabbinic discussions. In this compilation, conflicting opinions of the early scholars are contrasted, unusual words are explained and anonymous opinions are identified. Frequently, individual teachers cite specific cases to support their views and hypothetical eventualities are examined to reach a solution. Debates between outstanding scholars in one generation are often cited, as are differences of opinion between contemporary members of an academy of a teacher and his students. The range of talmudic exploration is much broader than that of the Mishnah and includes a wide range of rabbinic teachings about such subjects as theology, philosophy and ethics.

The Talmud

The Jerusalem Talmud was compiled at the end of the fourth century CE, and the Babylonian Talmud during the sixth century CE. Both record discussions of scholars on the Mishnah and are vast compendia of law, theology, ethics, legend and magic. An example of Talmudic discussion concerns the kinds of work forbidden on the Sabbath:

Mishnah: The main kinds of work are forty minus one.
Talmud: Why is the number stated? R. Jonahan said: So that if a man performs them all in a single state of ignorance, he is guilty on account of each one separately ...

Again they sat and thought: Concerning what we have learned, the main kinds of work are forty minus one – to what do they correspond?

R. Hanina b. Hama said to them: To the forms of work in the Tabernacle.

R. Jonathan son of R. Eleazar said: Thus R. Simeon b. R. Jose b. Lakonia used to say: They correspond to 'work', 'his work' and 'the work of', which can be found forty times minus one in the Torah.

R. Joseph asked: Is the verse 'And he went into the house to do work' (Genesis 39:11) to be included in this total or not?

Abbaye answered him: Bring out the scroll of the Law and we will count!

Rabbah b. Bar Hanina used to say in R. Johanan's name: They did not move from there until they brought a scroll of the Law and counted.[2]

Judaism in the Middle Ages

By the sixth century the Jews had become largely a diaspora people. Despite the loss of a homeland, they were unified by a common heritage: law, liturgy and shared traditions bound together the scattered communities stretching from Spain to Persia and Poland to Africa. Though the Middle Ages saw the formation of subcultures that could have divided the Jewish world, Jews remained united in their hope for messianic redemption, the restoration of the Holy Land, and an ingathering of the exiles. Living amongst Christians and Muslims, the Jewish community was reduced to a minority group and its marginal status resulted in repeated persecution. Though there were times of tolerance and creative activity, the threats of exile and death were always present in Jewish consciousness during this period.

Within the Islamic world, Jews along with Christians were recognized as 'Peoples of the Book' and were guaranteed religious toleration, judicial autonomy and exemption from the military. In turn they were required to accept the supremacy of the Islamic state. Such an arrangement was formally codified by the Pact of Omar dating from about 800 CE. According to this treaty, Jews were restricted in a number of spheres: they were not allowed to build houses of worship, make converts, carry weapons or ride horses. In addition, they were required to wear distinctive clothing and pay a yearly poll tax. Jewish farmers were also obliged to pay a land tax consisting of a portion of their produce. Despite these conditions, Jewish life prospered. In various urban centres many Jews were employed in crafts such as tanning, dyeing, weaving, silk manufacture and metal work; other Jews participated in inter-regional trade and established networks of agents and representatives.

Pact of Omar

The Pact of Omar is a treaty listing privileges and limitations entered into between conquering Muslims and those they had vanquished. Although this treaty was made between Muslims and Christians, its provisions applied to Jews as well:

> In the name of God, the Merciful, and the Compassionate! This is a writing to Omar from the Christians of such and such a city. When you [Muslims] marched against us [Christians], we asked of you protection for ourselves, our posterity, our possessions, and our co-religionists; and we made this stipulation with you, that we will not erect in our city or the suburbs any new monastery, church, cell or hermitage; that we will not repair any of such buildings that may fall into ruins, or renew those that may be situated in the Muslim quarters of the town; that we will not refuse the Muslims entry into our churches either by night or by day; that we will open the gates wide to passengers and travellers; that we will receive any Muslim traveller into our houses and give him food and lodging for three nights; that we will not harbour any spy in our churches or houses, or conceal any enemy of the Muslims.
>
> That we will not teach our children the Qur'an; that we will not make a show of the Christian religion nor invite any one to embrace it; that we will not prevent any of our kinsmen embracing Islam, if they so desire. That we will honour the Muslims and rise up in our assemblies when they wish to take their seats; that we will not imitate them in our dress, either in the cap, turban, sandals, or parting of the hair; that we will not make use of their expressions of speech, nor adopt their surnames; that we will not ride on saddles, or gird on swords, or take to ourselves arms or wear them, or engrave Arabic inscriptions on our rings;

that we will not sell wine; that we will shave the front of our heads; that we will keep to our own style of dress, wherever we may be; that we will wear girdles round our waists.[3]

During the first two centuries of Islamic rule under the Ummayad and Abbasid caliphates, Muslim leaders confirmed the authority of traditional Babylonian institutions. When the Arabs conquered Babylonia, they officially recognized the position of the exilarch, who for centuries had been the ruler of Babylonian Jewry. By the Abbasid period, the exilarch shared his power with the heads of the rabbinic academies, which had for centuries been the major centres of rabbinic learning. The head of each academy was known as the gaon, who delivered lectures as well as learned opinions on legal matters.

During the eighth century, messianic movements appeared in the Persian Jewish community which led to armed uprisings against Muslim authorities. Such revolts were quickly crushed, but an even more serious threat to traditional Jewish life was posed later in the century by the emergence of an anti-rabbinic sect, the Karaites. This group was founded in Babylonia in the 760s by Anan ben David. The guiding interpretative principle formulated by Anan, 'Search thoroughly in Scripture and do not rely on my opinion', was intended to point to Scripture itself as a source of law. After the death of the founder, new parties within the Karaite movement soon emerged, and by the tenth century Karaite communities were established in Israel, Iraq and Persia. The growth of Karaism provoked the rabbis to attack it as a heretical movement since these various groups rejected rabbinic law and formulated their own legislation.

Anan ben David

Different accounts are given of the origin of Anan ben David. According to the Jewish scholar Saadiah Gaon:

Anan had a younger brother called Hananiah. Although Anan was older in age and had a greater understanding of the Torah, the sages of that time were unwilling to elect him as exilarch because of his persistent unruliness and irreverence which were an inherent part of his character. So the sages chose Hananiah his brother, who was exceedingly modest and shy and who feared God greatly, and made him exilarch. Then Anan was

furious together with every scoundrel who still held the
Sadducean and Boethusian opinion and he decided to cause a
schism because he was frightened of the government of the
time. These heretics appointed Anan as their exilarch.[4]

By the eighth century the Muslim Empire began to undergo a process
of disintegration – this was accompanied by a decentralization of rabbinic
Judaism. The academies of Babylonia began to lose their hold on the
Jewish scholarly world, and in many places rabbinic schools were established in which rabbinic sources were studied. The growth of these local
centres of scholarship enabled individual teachers to exert their influence
on Jewish learning independently of the academies of Sura and
Pumbeditha. In the Holy Land, Tiberias was the location of an important
rabbinical academy as well as the centre of the masoretic scholars who
produced the standard text of the Bible. In Egypt, Kairouan and Fez
became centres of scholarship. But it was in Spain that the Jewish
community attained the greatest level of achievement in literature,
philosophy, theology and mysticism.

In their campaigns, Muslims did not manage to conquer all of Europe
– many countries remained under Christian rule, as did much of the
Byzantine Empire. In Christian Europe, Jewish study took place in a
number of important towns such as Mainz and Worms in the Rhineland
and Troyes and Sens in northern France. In such an environment the
study of the Talmud reached great heights: in Germany and northern
France scholars known as 'the tosafists' utilized new methods of talmudic
interpretation. In addition, Ashkenazic Jews of this period composed
religious poetry modelled on the liturgical compositions of fifth- and
sixth-century Israel.

Despite such an efflorescence of Jewish life, the expulsion of Jews from
countries in which they lived became a dominant policy of Christian
Europe. In 1182 the King of France expelled all Jews from the royal
domains near Paris, cancelled nearly all Christian debts to Jewish money-
lenders, and confiscated Jewish property. Although the Jews were recalled
in 1198, they were burdened with an additional royal tax and in the next
century they increasingly became the property of the king. In thirteenth-
century England the Jews were continuously taxed and the entire Jewish
population was expelled in 1290, as was that in France some years later.
At the end of the thirteenth century the German Jewish community
suffered violent attack. In the next century Jews were blamed for bringing
about the Black Death by poisoning the wells of Europe, and from 1348–9

Jews in France, Switzerland, Germany and Belgium suffered at the hands of their Christian neighbours. In the following two centuries massacres of Jews became a frequent occurrence. During this period the major mystical work of Spanish Jewry, the *Zohar*, was composed by Moses de Leon.

Profanation of the Host

Throughout the Middle Ages, Jews were accused of profaning the Host. As the twelfth-century chronicler of Liege, Jean d'Outremeuse, stated:

In this year, it happened at Cologne that the son of a converted Jew went on Easter Day to church, in order to receive the body of God. Along with others, he took it into his mouth and quickly bore it to his house; but when he returned from the church, he grew afraid and in his distress made a hole in the ground and buried the Host within it; but a priest came along, opened the hole, and in it found the shape of a child, which he intended to bear to the church. But there came from the sky a great light, the child was raised out of the priest's hands and borne up to heaven.[5]

Jewry in the Early Modern Period

By the end of the fourteenth century, political instability in Christian Europe led to the massacre of many Jewish communities in Castile and Aragon. Fearing for their lives, thousands of Jews converted to Christianity in 1391. Two decades later Spanish rulers introduced the Castilian laws, which segregated Jews from their Christian neighbours. In the following year a public disputation was held in Tortosa about the doctrine of the Messiah; as a result, increased pressure was applied to the Jewish population to convert. Those who became apostates (marranos) found life much easier, but by the fifteenth century, anti-Jewish sentiment again became a serious problem. In 1480 King Ferdinand and Queen Isabella established the Inquisition to determine whether former Jews practised Judaism in secret. In the late 1480s inquisitors used torture to extract confessions, and in 1492 the entire Jewish community was expelled from Spain. In the next century the Inquisition was established in Portugal.

The Spanish Expulsion

Initially, the Jewish community of Spain had enjoyed a measure of security, but in 1480 King Ferdinand and Queen Isabella brought the Inquisition to Spain and in 1492 the entire community was expelled:

In the year 5252 (1492), in the reign of King Ferdinand, the Lord afflicted the remnant of his people a second time and sent them into exile. The city of Granada had been captured by the king from the Moors and it had surrendered to him on 7th January. Then the King ordered the Jews to be expelled from the whole kingdom – from Castile, Catalonia, Aragon, Galicia, Majorca, Minorca, the Basque Provinces, the islands of Sardinia and Sicily and from the kingdom of Valencia. The Queen had already expelled them from Andalusia. The King granted them three months in which to leave.[6]

To escape such persecution many Spanish and Portuguese marranos sought refuge in various parts of the Ottoman Empire. Some of these Sephardic immigrants prospered and became part of the Ottoman court. Prominent among the rabbinic scholars of this period was Joseph ben Ephraim Caro, who emigrated from Spain to the Balkans. In the 1520s he commenced a study of Jewish law, *The House of Joseph*, based on previous codes of Jewish law; in addition he composed a shorter work, the *Shulhan Arukh*, which became the authoritative code of law in the Jewish world.

While working on the *Shulhan Arukh*, Caro emigrated to Safed in Israel, which had become a major centre of Jewish religious life. In the sixteenth century this small community had grown to a population of over 10,000 Jews. Here, talmudic academies were established and small groups engaged in the study of kabbalistic (mystical) literature as they piously awaited the coming of the Messiah. In this centre of kabbalistic activity, one of the greatest mystics of Safed, Moses Cordovero, collected, organized and interpreted the teachings of earlier mystical authors. Later in the sixteenth century, kabbalistic speculation was transformed by the greatest mystic of Safed, Isaac Luria.

Lurianic Kabbalah

Isaac Luria transformed the mystical tradition; his teachings were recorded by his disciple Hayyim Vital:

> Know that before the emanations were emanated and the creatures created, the supernal light of the Infinite filled everything there was. There was no empty area at all, no empty atmosphere, no vacuum. All was filled with that simple infinite light. It had neither beginning nor end. All was simple light in total sameness ... When in his simple will the Infinite resolved to create worlds and emanate the emanations, to bring to objective existence the perfection of his deeds, his names and his appellations, which was the reason for the creation of the world, he contracted in the middle point in himself, in the very centre ... After this contraction ... when there was left a vacuum, an empty atmosphere, through the mediation of the light of the Infinite, blessed be He, there was now available an area in which there could be the emanations, the beings created, formed and made.[7]

By the beginning of the seventeenth century, Lurianic mysticism had made an important impact on Sephardic Jews and messianic expectations had also become a central feature of Jewish life. In this milieu, the arrival of a self-proclaimed messianic king, Shabbatai Zevi, brought about a transformation of Jewish life and thought. After living in various cities, he travelled to Gaza where he encountered Nathan of Gaza, who believed Shabbatai was the Messiah. In 1665 his messiahship was proclaimed and Nathan sent letters to Jews in the diaspora asking them to recognize Shabbatai Zevi as their redeemer. The following year Shabbatai journeyed to Constantinople; on the order of the grand vizier he was arrested and put in prison. Eventually, he was brought to court and given the choice between conversion and death. In the face of this alternative, he converted to Islam. Such an act of apostasy scandalized most of his followers, but others continued to revere him as the Messiah. In the following century the most important Shabbatean sect was led by Jacob Frank, who believed himself to be the incarnation of Shabbatai.

Shabbatai Zevi

Shabbetai Zevi was seen by many throughout the Jewish world as the Messiah. The following contemporary account gives an idea of the excitement he inspired:

Millions of people were possessed when Shabbatai Zevi first appeared at Smyrna, and published himself to the Jews for their Messiah, relating the greatness of their approaching kingdom, the strong hand whereby God was about to deliver them from bondage, and gather them from all parts of the world. It was strange to see how this fancy took and how fast the report of Shabbatai and his doctrine flew through all parts where Jews inhabited and so deeply possessed them with a belief of their new kingdom and riches, and many of them with promotion to offices of government, renown and greatness; that in all places from Constantinople to Budu I perceived a strange transport in the Jews, none of them attending to any business, unless to wind up former negotiations and to prepare themselves and their families for a journey to Jerusalem. All their discourses, their dreams and disposal of their affairs tended to no other design but a reestablishment in the Land of Promise, to greatness and glory, wisdom and doctrine of the Messiah.[8]

During this period Poland had become a great centre of scholarship. In Polish academies scholars collected together the legal interpretations of previous authorities and composed commentaries on the *Shulhan Arukh*. To regulate Jewish life in the country at large Polish Jews established regional federations that administered Jewish affairs. In the midst of this general prosperity, the Polish Jewish community was subject to a series of massacres carried out by the Cossacks of the Ukraine, Crimean Tartars and Ukrainian peasants. In 1648 Bogdan Chmielnicki was elected hetman of the Cossacks and instigated an insurrection against the Polish gentry. As administrators of noblemen's estates, Jews were slaughtered in the process.

As the century progressed, Jewish life in Poland became increasingly insecure. Nonetheless, the Jewish community increased in size considerably during the eighteenth century. In the 1730s and 1740s Cossacks invaded the Ukraine, robbing and murdering Jewish inhabitants, and finally butchering the Jewish community of Uman in 1768. In Lithuania, on the other hand, Jewish life flourished and Vilna became an important centre of Jewish learning. Here Elijah ben Solomon Zalman, the Vilna Gaon, lectured to disciples on a wide range of subjects and composed commentaries on rabbinic sources.

Elsewhere in Europe this period witnessed Jewish persecution and oppression. Despite positive contact between Italian humanists and Jews, Christian anti-Semitism frequently led to persecution and suffering. In the sixteenth century the Counter-Reformation Church attempted to isolate the Jewish community. The Talmud was burned in 1553, and two years later Pope Paul reinstated the segregationist edict of the Fourth Lateran Council, forcing Jews to live in ghettos and barring them from most areas of economic life. In addition, marranos who took up the Jewish tradition were burned at the stake, and Jews were expelled from most Church domains.

In Germany the growth of Protestantism frequently led to adverse conditions for the Jewish population. Though Martin Luther was initially well disposed to the Jews, he soon came to realize that the Jewish community was intent on remaining true to its faith. As a consequence he composed a virulent attack on the Jews. Nonetheless, some Jews, known as Court Jews, attained positions of great importance among the German nobility. A number of these favoured individuals were appointed by the rulers as chief elders of the Jewish community and acted as spokesmen and defenders of German Jewry.

Martin Luther

In 1542 Martin Luther published his pamphlet *Against the Jews and their Lies*. In this work, he attacked both Judaism and the Jewish people:

> Know, o adored Christ, and make no mistake, that aside from the Devil, you have no enemy more venomous, more desperate, more bitter, than a true Jew who truly seeks to be a Jew. Now whoever wishes to accept venomous serpents, desperate enemies of the Lord, and to honour them to let himself be robbed, pillaged, corrupted, and cursed by them, need only turn to the Jews.[9]

In Holland some Jews had also attained an important influence on trade and finance. By the mid-seventeenth century both marranos and Ashkenazi Jews came to Amsterdam and established themselves in various areas of economic activity. By the end of the century there were nearly 10,000 Jews in Amsterdam; there the Jewish community was employed on the stock exchange, in the sugar, tobacco and diamond trades, and in insurance, manufacturing, printing and banking. In this milieu Jewish cultural activity flourished: Jewish writers published works of drama, theology and mystical lore. Though Jews in Holland were not granted full rights as citizens, they nevertheless enjoyed religious freedom, personal protection and the liberty of participating in a wide range of economic affairs.

Jews in the Modern World

By the middle of the eighteenth century the Jewish community had suffered numerous waves of persecution and was deeply dispirited by the conversion of Shabbatai Zevi. In this environment the Hasidic movement grounded in kabbalah sought to revitalize Jewish life. The founder of this new sect was Israel ben Eliezer, known as the Baal Shem Tov (Besht). Born in southern Poland, he travelled to Medzibozh in Polodia, Russia, in the 1730s, where he performed various miracles and instructed his disciples in kabbalistic lore. By the 1740s he attracted a considerable number of disciples, who passed on his teaching. After his death, Dov Baer became the leader of this sect and Hasidism spread to southern Poland, the Ukraine and Lithuania. The growth of this movement engendered considerable hostility on the part of rabbinic authorities, and by the end of the century the Jewish religious establishment of Vilna denounced Hasidism to the Russian government.

Baal Shem Tov

The Baal Shem Tov taught that sincere devotion to God was to be valued above traditional rabbinic learning:

The Baal Shem Tov used to say: No child is born except as the result of joy and pleasure. In the same way, if a man wants his prayers to be heard, he must offer them up with joy and pleasure. The Baal Shem Tov used to say: Do not laugh at a man who gestures as he prays fervently. He gestures in order to keep himself from distracting thoughts which intrude upon him and threaten to drown his prayer. You would not laugh at a drowning man who gestures in the water in order to save himself. The Baal Shem Tov used to say: Sometimes a man becomes intoxicated with ecstasy when rejoicing over the law. He feels the love of God burning within him and the words of prayer come rushing out of his mouth. He must pray quickly to keep pace with them all.[10]

During the latter part of the century the treatment of Jews in Central Europe was less harsh due to the influence of Christian polemicists who argued that Jewish life should be improved. The Holy Roman Emperor Joseph II embraced such views; he abolished the Jewish badge as well as taxes imposed on Jewish travellers and proclaimed an edict of toleration that granted the Jews numerous rights. As in Germany, reformers in France during the 1770s and 1780s ameliorated the situation of the Jewish population. In 1789 the National Assembly issued a declaration stating that all human beings are born and remain free and equal and that no person should be persecuted for his opinions as long as they do not subvert civil law. In 1791 a resolution was passed that bestowed citizenship rights on all Jews. This change in Jewish status occurred elsewhere in Europe as well – in 1796 the Dutch Jews of the Batavian republic were granted full citizenship rights, and in 1797 the ghettos of Padua and Rome were abolished.

In 1799 Napoleon became the First Consul of France and five years later he was proclaimed emperor. Napoleon's Code of Civil Law propounded in 1804 established the right of all individuals to follow any trade and declared equality for all. After 1806 a number of German principalities were united in the French kingdom of Westphalia, where Jews were granted equal rights. In the same year Napoleon convened an Assembly of Jewish Notables to consider a number of religious issues. In the following year he summoned a Grand Sanhedrin consisting of rabbis and laymen to confirm the views of the Assembly. This body pledged its allegiance to the emperor and nullified any features of the Jewish tradition that conflicted with the particular requirements of citizenship.

After Napoleon's defeat and abdication, the map of Europe was redrawn by the Congress of Vienna between 1814–15, and in addition the diplomats at the Congress issued a resolution that instructed the German confederation to improve the status of the Jews. Yet despite this decree, the German government disowned the rights of equality that had previously been granted to Jews by the French. In 1830, however, a more liberal attitude prevailed, and various nations advocated a more tolerant approach. The

French Revolution of 1848, which led to revolutionary outbreaks in Prussia, Austria, Hungary, Italy and Bohemia, forced rulers to grant constitutions that guaranteed freedom of speech, assembly and religion.

Within this environment Jewish emancipation gathered force. At the end of the eighteenth century the Jewish philosopher Moses Mendelssohn advocated the modernization of Jewish life, and to further this advance he translated the Pentateuch into German so that Jews would be able to speak the language of the country in which they lived. Following Mendelssohn's example, a number of Prussian followers, the maskilim, fostered a Jewish Enlightenment – the Haskalah – which encouraged Jews to abandon medieval forms of life and thought. By the 1820s the centre of this movement shifted to the Austrian Empire, where journals propounding the ideas of the Enlightenment were published. In the 1840s the Haskalah spread to Russia, where writers made important contributions to Hebrew literature and translated textbooks and European fiction into Hebrew. This change in status of the Jewish community in the nineteenth century provides the background to the evolution of Jewish life in contemporary society.

Moses Mendelssohn

Moses Mendelssohn was the most important thinker of the Haskalah; he worked tirelessly for freedom of conscience of religion. Not only did he translate the Pentateuch into German, he also encouraged the modernization of Jewish education to include the teaching of secular culture. He advised other Jews:

> Adopt the customs and constitution of the country in which you live, but also be careful to follow the religion of your fathers. As well as you can you must carry both burdens. It is not easy because, on the one hand, people make it hard for you to carry the burden of civil life because of your faithfulness to your religion, and on the other hand, the climate of the times makes keeping religious law harder than it need be in some respects. Nevertheless you must try. Stand fast in the place you have been allocated by Providence and submit to everything that happens to you as you were commanded long ago by your lawgiver. Indeed, I do not understand how those who are part of the household of Jacob can with a good conscience not fully observe the Jewish law.[11]

Chapter 1

The Basics

According to tradition, the beginnings of the Jewish nation stemmed from God's revelation to Abraham at the beginning of the second millennium BCE. Known as Abram, he came from Ur of the Chaldeans, a Sumerian city of Mesopotamia. The Book of Genesis recounts that God called him to go to the land of Canaan: 'Go from your country and your kindred and your father's house to the land I will show you. And I will make of you a great nation' (Genesis 12:1–2). The Hebrew Bible traces the history of this tribe from patriarchal times to the Exodus from Egypt several centuries later, and eventually the conquest of the land of Canaan by Joshua in about 1200 BCE. In later books of the Bible, the period of the judges, the rise of the monarchy, the emergence of the prophets, and the eventual destruction of the Northern and Southern Kingdoms are described in detail. With the growth of rabbinic Judaism in the Hellenistic period, the Jewish faith underwent a fundamental change that profoundly transformed Jewish life until the present. This long history of the Jewish people – stretching back over nearly forty centuries – provides the historical framework for the central beliefs and practices of the Jewish religion.

The Fundamental Beliefs

l. The Unity of God: Throughout the history of the Jewish people, the belief in one God has served as the cardinal principle of the faith. From biblical times to the present, Jews daily recite the Shema prayer: 'Hear O Israel, the Lord our God, the Lord is One.' According to Scripture, God alone is to be worshipped. Continuing this tradition, the sages of the early rabbinic period stressed that any form of polytheistic belief is abhorrent. For thousands of years, Jews have proclaimed their belief and trust in the one God who created the universe and rules over creation. Such a claim is unconditional and absolute.

The Prophet Isaiah

In the sixth century BCE the prophet Isaiah proclaimed his conviction in the one true God:

I am the Lord, and there is no other,
besides me there is no God ...
I form light and create darkness,
I make weal and create woe,
I the Lord do all these things. (Isaiah 45:5a, 7)

---

2. Creation: According to Genesis 1, God created Heaven and Earth. This belief is a central feature of the synagogue service. In the synagogue hymn before the reading from the Psalms, for example, God is depicted as the creator of everything:

Blessed be He who spoke, and the world existed:
Blessed be He;
Blessed be He who was the master of the world in the beginning.[1]

In rabbinic literature scholars speculated about the nature of the creative process. In Genesis Rabbah (midrash on Genesis) for example, the idea of the world as a pattern in the mind of God is expressed in relation to the belief that God looked into the Torah and created the world. Here the Torah is conceived as a type of blueprint. In the Middle Ages, a number of Jewish theologians believed that God created the universe ex nihilo. The kabbalists, however, interpreted the doctrine of ex nihilo in a special sense. God, they maintained, should be understood as the Divine Nothing because, as He is in and of himself, nothing can be predicated. The Divine is beyond human understanding. Creation ex nihilo thus refers to the creation of the universe out of God, the Divine Nothing. This occurred, they argued, through a series of divine emanations.

3. Divine Transcendence and Immanence: For Jews, God is conceived as the transcendent creator of the Universe. Thus in Genesis 1:1–2, He is described as forming heaven and earth. Throughout Scripture this theme of divine transcendence is repeatedly affirmed. In the rabbinic period Jewish scholars formulated the doctrine of the Shekhinah to denote the

divine presence. Later in the Middle Ages the doctrine of the Shekhinah was further elaborated. According to the ninth-century scholar Saadiah Gaon, the Shekhinah is identical with the glory of God, which serves as an intermediary between God and human beings during the prophetic encounter. In kabbalistic writings the Shekhinah also played an important role. As the divine power closest to the created world, the Shekhinah is the medium through which divine light passes.

Levi Yitzhak of Berditchev

The song of the nineteenth-century Hasidic master, Levi Yitzhak of Berditchev, is characteristic of Jewish belief through the ages to the present:

Where I wander – You!
Where I ponder – You!
Only you. You again, always You!
You! You! You!
When I am gladdened – You!
When I am saddened – You!
Only You. You again, always You!
You! You! You![2]

---

4. Eternity: Throughout Scripture God is described as having neither beginning nor end. This biblical teaching was later elaborated by the rabbis. According to the Talmud there is an unbridgeable gap between God and human beings. In midrashic sources God's eternal reign is similarly affirmed. Thus when Pharaoh was told by Moses and Aaron in the name of God to let the people go, Pharaoh declared that God's name is not found in the list of gods. In reply Moses and Aaron declared: O fool! The dead can be sought among the living but how can the living be sought among the dead. Our God lives, but those you mention are dead. Our God is "the living God and the everlasting King"' (Jeremiah 10:10). In response Pharaoh asked whether this God was young or old, how old he was, how many cities he had conquered, how many provinces he had subdued, and how long he had been king. In reply Moses and Aaron proclaimed: 'The Power and might of our God fill the world. He was before the world was created and He will be when all the world comes to an end, and He has created thee and gave thee the spirit of life.'

5. Omnipotence and Omniscience: From biblical times the belief in God's omnipotence has been a central feature. Thus in the Book of Genesis, when Sarah expressed astonishment at the suggestion she should have a child at the age of 90, she was criticized: 'The Lord said to Abraham, "Why did Sarah laugh, and say 'Shall I indeed bear a child now that I am old? Is anything too hard for the Lord?"' (Genesis 18:13–14). Paralleling this belief, Jews throughout the ages have affirmed that God is all-knowing. Following the biblical view, rabbinic Judaism asserted that God's knowledge is not limited by space and time. Rather, nothing is hidden from him.

Exodus Rabbah

According to the midrash, God is capable not only of doing every-thing, but of doing so simultaneously:

God spoke all these things saying (Exodus 20:1). God can do everything simultaneously. He kills and makes alive at one and the same movement; He strikes and heals; the prayer of the woman in travail, of them who are upon the sea or in the desert, or who are bound in the prison; He hears them all at once; whether men are in the east or west, north or south, He hearkens to all at once.[3]

---

6. Providence: In the Bible, the notion that God controls and guides the universe is an essential belief. According to Scripture, there are two types of providence: (1) general providence – God provision for the world in general; and (2) special providence – God's care for each individual. God's general providence was manifest in his freeing the ancient Israelites from Egyptian bondage and guiding them to the Promised Land. The belief in the unfolding of his plan for salvation is a further illustration of such provi-dential care for his creatures. Linked to this concern for all is God's provi-dential concern for every person. In the words of Jeremiah: 'I know, O Lord, that the way of man is not in himself, that it is not in man who walks to direct his steps (Jeremiah 10:23). Subsequently, the doctrine of divine providence was elaborated in rabbinic sources. The Mishnah declares: 'Everything is foreseen.' In the Talmud we read: 'No man suffers so much as the injury of a finger when it has been decreed in heaven.'

7. Divine Goodness: 'According to the Hebrew Bible, God is the all-good ruler of the universe. In rabbinic literature, He has chosen Israel as his

messenger to all peoples – as creator and redeemer, He is the father to all. Such affirmations about God's goodness have given rise to intense speculation about the mystery of evil. In Scripture the authors of Job and Ecclesiastes explored the question why the righteous suffer, and this quest continued into the rabbinic period. Yet it was not until the Middle Ages that Jewish thinkers began to wrestle with the philosophical perplexities connected with the existence of evil. For the kabbalists, the existence of human suffering constituted a central problem of the Jewish faith. According to one tradition, evil has no objective reality. Human beings are unable to receive all the influx from the sefirot (divine emanations), and it is this inability that is the origin of evil. Another view depicts the sefirah (divine emanation) of power as an attribute whose name is evil. On the basis of such a teaching, Isaac the Blind in the thirteenth century concluded that there must be a positive root of evil and death.

8. Revelation: According to tradition, the entire Torah (Five Books of Moses) was communicated by God to the Jewish people. In the twelfth century the Jewish philosopher Moses Maimonides formulated this belief as one of the cardinal principles of the faith:

> The Torah was revealed from Heaven. This implies our belief that the whole of the Torah found in our hands this day is the Torah that was handed down by Moses, and that it is all of divine origin. By this I mean that the whole of the Torah came unto him from before God in a manner which is metaphorically called 'speaking'; but the real nature of that communication is unknown to everybody except to Moses to whom it came.[4]

In rabbinic literature a distinction is drawn between the revelation of the Five Books of Moses and the prophetic writings. This is expressed by saying that the Torah was given directly by God, whereas the prophetic books were given by means of prophecy. The remaining books of the Bible were conveyed by means of the Holy Spirit rather than through prophecy. Nonetheless, all these writings constitute the canon of Scripture. According to the rabbis, the expositions and elaborations of the Written Law were also revealed by God to Moses on Mount Sinai. Subsequently, they were passed on from generation to generation, and through this process additional legislation was incorporated. Thus traditional Judaism affirms that God's revelation was twofold and binding for all time.

9. Torah and Commandments: According to tradition, God revealed 613 commandments (mitzvot) to Moses on Mount Sinai; they are recorded in the Five Books of Moses. These prescriptions, which are to be observed

as part of God's covenant with Israel, are classified in two major categories: (1) statutes concerned with ritual performances characterized as obligations between human beings and God; and (2) judgements consisting of ritual laws that would have been adopted by society even if they had not been decreed by God (such as laws regarding murder and theft). These 613 commandments consist of 365 negative (prohibited) and 248 positive (duties to be performed) prescriptions.

Traditional Judaism maintains that Moses received the Oral Torah in addition to the Written Law. This was passed down from generation to generation and was the subject of rabbinic debate. The first authoritative compilation of the Oral Law was the Mishnah composed by Judah Ha-Nasi in the second century CE. In subsequent centuries sages continued to discuss the content of Jewish law: their deliberations are recorded in the Palestinian and Babylonian Talmuds. Subsequently, rabbinic authorities continued the development of Jewish law by issuing answers to specific questions. In time various scholars felt the need to produce codes of Jewish law so that all members of the community would have access to the legal tradition.

10. Sin and Repentance: In the Bible, sin is understood as a transgression of God's decree. According to rabbinic Judaism, sins can be classified according to their gravity as indicated by the punishments prescribed by biblical law. The more serious the punishment, the more serious the offence. A distinction is also drawn between sins against other human beings and offences against God alone. Sins against God can be atoned for by repentance, prayer, and giving charity. In cases of offence against others, however, such acts require restitution and placation as a condition for atonement.

Yom Kippur

On the Day of Atonement (Yom Kippur) the faithful are to repent of their sins and ask God for forgiveness:

Our God and God of our fathers, hear our prayer; do not ignore our plea. We are neither so brazen nor so arrogant to claim that we are righteous, without sin, for indeed we have sinned.

We abuse, we betray, we are cruel. We destroy, we embitter, we falsify. We gossip, we hate, we insult. We jeer, we kill, we lie. We mock, we neglect, we oppress. We pervert, we quarrel, we rebel. We steal, we transgress, we are unkind. We are violent, we are wicked, we are xenophobic. We yield to evil, we are zealots for bad causes ... May it therefore be your will, Lord our God and God of our fathers, to forgive us all our sins, to pardon our iniquities, to grant us atonement for all our transgressions.[5]

11. Chosen People: The concept of Israel as God's chosen people has been a constant feature of Jewish thought from biblical times to the present. Through its election Israel has been given a historic mission to bear divine truth to humanity. Divine choice demands reciprocal response. Israel is obligated to keep God's statutes and observe his laws. In doing so, the nation will be able to persuade the nations of the world that there is only one universal God. Israel is to be a prophet to the nations, in that it will bring them to salvation. In rabbinic sources the biblical doctrine of the chosen people is a constant theme. While upholding the belief that God chose the Jews from all peoples, the rabbis argued that their election was due to an acceptance of the Torah. According to the rabbis, there is a special relationship between the children of Israel and God based on love – this is the basis of the allegorical interpretations in rabbinic sources of the Song of Songs and it is also expressed in the Talmud by such sayings as: 'How beloved is Israel before the Holy One, blessed be He; for wherever they were exiled the Shekhinah (divine presence) was with them.' Rabbinic literature also emphasizes that God's election of the Jewish people is due to the character of the nation and of the patriarchs in particular; according to the Talmud, mercy and forgiveness are characteristic of Abraham and his descendants.

Prayer Book

The Kiddush prayer for the Sabbath refers to God's choice of Israel as his people:

Blessed art thou, O Lord our God, king of the universe, who has hallowed us by thy commandments and hast taken pleasure in us, and in love and favour hast given us thy holy Sabbath as an inheritance, a memorial of the creation – that day being also the first of the holy convocations, in remembrance of the departure from Egypt. For thou hast chosen us and hallowed us above all nations, and in love and favour hast given us thy holy Sabbath as an inheritance. Blessed art thou, O Lord, who hallowest the Sabbath.[6]

12. Promised Land: Throughout their history the Jewish people have longed for a land of their own. In Genesis God called Abraham to travel to Canaan, where he promised to make him a great nation. This same declaration was made to his grandson Jacob who, after wrestling with God's messenger, was renamed Israel (meaning 'he who struggles with God'). After Jacob's son Joseph became a vizier in Egypt, the Israelite clan settled in Egypt for several hundred years. Eventually Moses led them out of Egyptian bondage, and the people settled in the Promised Land. There they established a monarchy but, due to the corruption of the nation, God punished his chosen people through the instrument of foreign powers, which devastated the Northern Kingdom in the eighth century BCE and the Southern Kingdom two centuries later.

Though the Temple lay in ruins and Jerusalem was destroyed, Jews who had been exiled to Babylonia had not lost their faith in God. Sustained by their belief that God would deliver them from exile, a number of Jews sought permission to return to their former home. In 538 BCE King Cyrus of Persia allowed them to leave, and under the leadership of Joshua and Zerubbabel restoration of the Temple began. Centuries later, however, the Temple was destroyed by the Romans and the Jews were bereft of a homeland. The glories of ancient Israel had come to an end, and the Jews were destined to live among the nations. In their despair the nation longed for a messianic figure of the House of David who would lead them back to Zion. Basing their beliefs on prophecies in Scripture, they foresaw a period of redemption in which earthly life would be transformed and all nations would bow down to the one true God. Such a vision animated rabbinic reflection about God's providential plan for his chosen people.

Psalms of Solomon

The Psalms of Solomon extol the messianic king who will rebuild the land and draw all nations to Zion:

He shall gather together a holy people whom he shall lead in righteousness. And he shall judge the tribes of the people that has been sanctified by the Lord his God … And he shall divide them according to their tribes upon the land. And neither sojourner nor alien shall sojourn with them any more. He shall judge peoples and nations in the wisdom of his righteousness. Selah. The people of the nations shall serve him under his yoke: He shall glorify the Lord openly in all the earth; And he shall purge Jerusalem making it holy as of old. So that nations shall come from all the ends of the earth to see his glory. (Psalms of Solomon 17:26, 28–31a)[7]

13. Prayer: According to the Jewish tradition, human beings are able to communicate with God individually or collectively; in response, God answers the prayers that are addressed to him. In Scripture He is portrayed as a personal Deity who created human beings in his image; as a consequence, they are able to attain this exalted position. The Bible itself lists more than eighty examples of both formalized and impromptu worship. Initially, no special prayers were required for regular prayer, but later, worship services became institutionalized through sacrifices and offerings. In ancient Israel three types of sacrifice were offered in the Temple: animal sacrifice made as a burnt offering for sin, meal offerings, and libations. The rituals and practices prescribed for the Temple sacrifice are set down in Leviticus chapters 2 and 23 and Numbers chapters 28 and 29.

The Mishnah states that priests serving in the Second Temple participated in a short liturgy comprising the Shema (Deuteronomy 6:4), the Ten Commandments and the Priestly Blessing (Numbers 6:24–6). During this period the entire congregation began to pray at fixed times, and an order of prayers has been attributed to the men of the Great Assembly. Regular services were held four times daily by the delegations of representatives from the 24 districts of the country. These services were referred to as: shaharit (morning), musaf (additional), minhah (afternoon), and neilat shearim (evening). Several orders of prayers coexisted until Gamaliel II produced a regularized standard after the destruction of the Temple in 70 CE. Prayers then officially replaced the sacrifices that could no longer be made. This new ritual, referred to as 'service of the heart', was conducted in the synagogue.

Shema

The Shema is a central prayer of the Jewish liturgy. It is made up of three passages: Deuteronomy 6:4–9; Deuteronomy 11:13–21; Numbers

15:37–41. Recited every day, the first paragraph contains the phrase, 'Hear, O Israel, the Lord is our God, the Lord is One':

Hear, O Israel, the Lord is Our God, the Lord is One. Blessed be his name, whose glorious kingdom is for ever and ever. And thou shalt love the Lord thy God with all thine heart, and with all thy soul, and with all thy might. And these words which I command this day, shall be upon thine heart and thou shalt teach them diligently unto thy children, and shalt talk of them when thou sittest in thine house, and when thou walkest by the way, and when thou liest down, and when thou risest up. And thou shalt bind them for a sign upon thine hand, and they shall be for frontlets between thine eyes. And thou shalt write them upon the door-posts of thy house and upon thy gates.[8]

14. Love and Fear of God: Within the Jewish faith, the love of God is of central importance. Thus Deuteronomy declares: 'You shall love the Lord your God with all your heart and with all your soul and with all your might' (Deuteronomy 6:5). In the Mishnah this verse is quoted to demonstrate that human beings must love God not only for the good that befalls them, but for the evil as well. This explanation is based on an interpretation of three expressions in this verse: 'with all your heart' means with both the good and evil inclinations; 'with all your soul' means even if God takes away your soul through martyrdom; 'with all your might' means with all your wealth. According to the Mishnah the injunction to love God involves being faithful even if this requires the loss of one's wealth or one's life.

In rabbinic sources loving God is perceived as living according to his decrees. Among medieval Jewish thinkers, however, stress was placed on mystical love. Thus in *The Book of Beliefs and Opinions*, the ninth-century Jewish philosopher Saadiah Gaon asks how it is possible to have knowledge of God, much less love him, since we have not perceived him with our senses. In response, he asserts that certain statements are believed as true even though they cannot be proved on empirical grounds. According to Saadiah, it is possible to acquire knowledge of God through rational speculation and the miracles afforded by Scripture. Hence truth about God is able to mingle with the human spirit.

In *Duties of the Heart*, the eleventh-century Jewish philosopher Bahya ibn Pakuda sees the love of God as the final goal – this is the aim of all virtues. However, the only way is through fear of him. For Bahya such fear involves abstinence from worldly desires. When human beings contemplate God's power and greatness, they bow before his majesty until God stills this fear. Individuals who love God in this fashion have no other interest than serving him. In this regard Bahya quotes the saint who used to proclaim at night: 'My God! Thou hast made me hungry and left me naked. Thou hast caused me to dwell in night's darkness and hast shown me thy power and might. Yet even if thou wouldst burn me in fire, I would continue only to love thee and rejoice in thee.'

15. Messiah: The term 'Messiah' is an adaptation of the Hebrew Ha-Mashiah (the Anointed), a term frequently used in Scripture. In the Second Book of Samuel the view was expressed that the Lord had chosen David and his descendants to reign over Israel to the end of time. With the fall of the Davidic Empire after Solomon's death, there arose the view that the house of David would eventually rule over the two divided kingdoms as well as neighbouring peoples. Such an expectation paved the way for the vision of a transformation of earthly life. During this time there was intense speculation about the nature of the Messiah. In the Book of Zechariah, for example, two messianic figures are depicted. Later, among the Dead Sea sect, these two figures were joined by a third personage, the prophet of the latter days.

Despite such a proliferation of messianic figures, it was the Davidic Messiah who came to dominate Jewish thought. According to tradition, this king-Messiah will put an end to all wars on earth, make a covenant with the righteous and slay the wicked. Such a conviction served as the basis for subsequent rabbinic reflection about messianic redemption, the ingathering of the exiles, and salvation in the World-to-Come. As time passed, the rabbis elaborated the themes found in the Bible and Jewish literature of the Second Temple period. In the midrashim and the Talmud they formulated an elaborate eschatological scheme divided into various stages. In their depiction of the Messiah, scholars formulated the doctrine of another Messiah, the son of Joseph, who would precede the king-Messiah, the Messiah ben David. According to legend, this Messiah will engage in battle with Gog and Magog, the enemies of Israel, and be slain. Only after this will the Messiah ben David arrive in glory.

16. Afterlife: Though there is no explicit reference to the hereafter in the Hebrew Bible, a number of expressions are used to refer to the realm of the dead. Though such references point to a biblical conception of an afterlife, there is no indication of a clearly defined concept. It was only later in the Graeco-Roman world that such a notion began to take shape. The idea of a future world in which the righteous would be compensated for the ills they suffered in this life was prompted a failure to justify the

ways of God by any other means. According to biblical theology, individuals were promised rewards for obeying God's law and punishments were threatened for disobedience. As time passed, however, it became clear that life did not operate in accordance with such a tidy scheme. In response to this dilemma, the rabbis developed a doctrine of reward and punishment in the hereafter. Such a belief helped Jews to cope with suffering in this life, and it also explained, if not the presence of evil in the world, then at least the value of creation despite the world's ills.

According to rabbinic Judaism, the World-to-Come (Olam Ha-Ba) is divided into several stages, beginning with the time of messianic redemption. According to the Talmud, this is to take place on earth after a period of calamity. Peace will reign throughout nature; Jerusalem will be rebuilt; and at the close of this era, the dead will be resurrected and rejoined with their souls, and a final judgement will come upon all humanity. Those who are judged righteous will enter into heaven whereas the wicked will be punished everlastingly.

Basic Practices

1. Places of Worship: Scripture relates that Moses made a portable shrine, following God's instructions. This structure travelled with the Israelites in the desert and was placed in the centre of the camp in an open courtyard. The fence surrounding it consisted of wooden pillars from which a cloth curtain was suspended. Located in the eastern half of the courtyard, the sanctuary measured 30 by 10 cubits (a cubit being roughly 18 inches). At its end stood the Holy of Holies, which was separated by a veil hanging on five wooden pillars on which were woven images of the cherubim. Inside the Holy of Holies was the Ark of the Covenant, the table on which the shewbread was placed, the incense altar, and the menorah (candelabrum). In the courtyard there was also an outer altar on which sacrifices were made, as well as a brass laver for priests.

Eventually, this structure was superseded by the Temple, which was built by Solomon in Jerusalem in the tenth century BCE. Standing within a royal compound – which also consisted of the palace, a Hall of Judgement, the Hall of Cedars, and a house for Solomon's wife – the Temple was 60 cubits long, 20 cubits wide, and 30 cubits high. The main building consisted of the Holy of Holies. Within the Holy of Holies stood the Ark, which contained the Two Tablets of the Covenant on which the Ten Commandments were written. From the time of Solomon's reign, the Temple served as the site for prayer and the offering of sacrifices to God.

However, alongside the Temple, the synagogue also functioned as a place of worship. After the exile in the sixth century BCE, Jews in Babylonia established this institution for public worship, Jews coming together in synagogues to study and pray. On their return to Jerusalem in the latter part of the sixth century BCE, the Jewish populace continued to gather in synagogues as well as offering sacrifices in the Temple. Since the Temple's destruction in 70 CE, however, synagogues have served as the only places of worship up until the present day.

Synagogue

God's presence was manifest in the synagogue, where periods for daily prayer were fixed:

'My love is like a gazelle' (Song of Songs 2:9). As the gazelle leaps from place to place, and from fence to fence, and from tree to tree, so God jumps and leaps from synagogue to synagogue to bless the children of Israel.[9]

---

2. Worship: For the Jewish people, prayer served as the vehicle by which they expressed their joys, sorrows and hopes. It has played a major role in the religious life of the nation, especially in view of the successive crises and calamities in which the Jews have been involved throughout their history. In such situations Jews continually turned to God for assistance. In additional to personal prayer, Jews have prayed communally. In ancient times Jewish communal worship centred on the Temple in Jerusalem. With the destruction of the Second Temple in 70 CE, sacrificial offerings were replaced by the prayer service in the synagogue. To enhance uniformity, fixed periods for daily prayer were introduced, the times of which corresponded to those when sacrifices had been offered in the Temple. By the time of completion of the Talmud in the sixth century, the essential features of the synagogue service were established, but it was only in the eighth century that the first prayer book was composed by Rav Amram, Gaon of Sura.

In the order of service the first central feature is the Shema. In accordance with the commandment 'You shall talk of them when you lie down and when you arise' (Deuteronomy 6:7), Jews are commanded to recite this prayer during the morning and evening service. The second major feature of the synagogue service is the Amidah (Eighteen Benedictions). These prayers were composed over a long period of time and received their full form in the second century. They consist of 18 separate prayers plus an additional benediction dealing with heretics. From earliest times the Torah was read in public gatherings; subsequently, regular readings of the Torah on Sabbaths and festivals were instituted. Other features of the synagogue service are the kaddish prayer, which takes several forms, and the Hallel, consisting of Psalms 113–18. Since the thirteenth century, the three daily services have concluded with the recitation of the Alenu prayer, which proclaims God as king.

3. Sabbath: Genesis 2:1–3 declares: 'The heavens and the earth were finished, and all the host of them. And on the seventh day God finished his work which he had done, and He rested on the seventh day from all his work which He had done. So God blessed the seventh day and hallowed it, because on it God rested from all his work which He had done in creation.' This passage serves as the basis for the decree that no work should be done on the Sabbath day. During their sojourn in the wilderness of Zin, the Israelites were first commanded to observe the Sabbath. They were told to work on five days of the week when they should collect a single portion of manna; on the sixth day they were instructed to collect a double portion for the following day, which was to be a 'day of solemn rest, a holy sabbath of the Lord' (Exodus 16:23).

By the time the Sanhedrin began to function, the observance of the Sabbath was regulated by Jewish law. Following the injunction of Exodus 20:10, the primary aim was to refrain from work. In the Torah only a few provisions are delineated: kindling a fire, ploughing and harvesting, carrying from one place to another. Such regulations were expanded by the rabbis, who listed 39 categories of work (which were involved in the building of the Tabernacle). In the Talmud these categories were discussed and expanded to include within each category a range of activities. In order to ensure that individuals did not transgress these prescriptions, the rabbis enacted further legislation, which serves as a fence around the law.

The Sabbath itself commences on Friday at sunset. A little while before sunset Sabbath candles are traditionally lit by the woman of the house, who recites the relevant blessing. In the synagogue, the service preceding Friday maariv takes place at twilight. Traditionally, when the father returns home from the synagogue, he blesses the children. At the Sabbath table, the father recites the kiddush prayer over a cup of wine. This is followed by the washing of the hands and the blessing of bread. The meal is followed by the singing of hymns (zemirot) and concludes with the Grace after Meals. On Sabbath morning, there is a special liturgy consisting of a morning service, the reading of the Torah and the Haftarah (reading from the prophets), and the additional service. At the end of the Sabbath, the evening service takes place and is followed by the Havdalah service.

Lekhah Dodi

The Lekhah Dodi (Come my beloved) prayer is recited in anticipation of the coming of the Sabbath:

Come, my beloved, with chorus of praise, Welcome Bride Sabbath, the Queen of days.
   'Keep and Remember'! – in one divine word, He that is one, made his will heard; One is the name of him, one is the Lord! His are the fame and the glory and praise!
   Sabbath, to welcome thee, joyful we haste, Fountain of blessing from ever thou wast – First in God's planning thou fashioned the last, Crown of his handiwork, chiefest of days …[10]

---

4. Pilgrim Festivals: According to the Book of Deuteronomy, Jews are to celebrate three pilgrim festivals each year: 'Three times each year shall all your males appear before the Lord your God at the place which He will choose, at the feast of unleavened bread, at the feast of weeks, and at the feast of booths' (Deuteronomy 16:16). The first of these festivals is Passover (Pesach) which is celebrated for eight days from the 15th to the 22nd of Nisan.

a. Pesach (Passover): Passover commemorates the Exodus from Egypt. In preparation for this festival, Jewish law stipulates that all leaven must be removed from the house. On the night before the 14th of Nisan a formal search is made for any remains of leaven. This is then put aside and burned on the following morning. The first night of Passover is celebrated in the home ceremony referred to as the seder. This is done to fulfil the biblical commandment to relate the story of the Exodus to one's son. The symbols placed on the seder table serve to remind those present of Egyptian bondage, God's redemption, and the celebration in Temple times. They include matzah (unleavened bread), four cups of wine, the cup of Elijah, bitter herbs, parsley, haroset (mixture of apples, nuts, cinnamon and wine), a roasted shank-bone, a roasted egg, and salt water.

b. Shavuot (Festival of Weeks): This festival is celebrated for two days on the 6th and 7th of Sivan and commemorates the giving of the law on Mount Sinai. Synagogues are traditionally decorated with flowers or plants, and dairy food is consumed during the festival.

c. Sukkot (Booths): The third pilgrim festival commemorates God's protection of the Israelites during their sojourn in the desert. Leviticus commands that Jews are to construct booths during this period as a reminder that the people of Israel dwelt in booths when they fled from Egypt (Leviticus 23:42–3). During this festival a sukkah (booth) is constructed and its roof is covered with branches of trees and plants. For the duration of Sukkot, meals are to be eaten inside the sukkah. On each day of the seven days of the festival, beginning on the 15th of Tishri, the lulav (palm branch) is waved in every direction, symbolizing God's presence throughout the world. Holding the four species (palm, myrtle, willow and citron), Jews make one circuit around the Torah which is carried onto the bimah (platform) on the first six days. During this circuit hoshanah prayers are recited. In conformity with Leviticus 23:36 ('On the eighth day you shall hold a holy convocation ... it is a solemn assembly'), Shemini Atzeret and Simhat Torah are celebrated following the festival.

5. New Year and Day of Atonement: In ancient times the Jewish New Year (Rosh Hashanah) took place on one day; it is presently observed for two days on the 1st and 2nd of Tishri, marking the beginning of the Ten Days of Penitence, which end on the Day of Atonement (Yom Kippur).

a. New Year: According to the Mishnah, all human beings will pass before God on the New Year; the Talmud expands this idea by stressing the need for self-examination. In rabbinic literature each person stands before the Throne of God, and judgement on every person is entered on the New Year and sealed on the Day of Atonement. On Rosh Hashanah the Ark curtain, reading desk and Torah Scroll mantles are decked in white, and the rabbi, cantor and person who blows the shofar (ram's horn) all wear a white robe (kittle). During the service the shofar is repeatedly sounded, calling sinners to repent. Traditionally, it was a custom to go to the seaside or the banks of a river on the afternoon of the first day to perform the ceremony of Tashlikh, which symbolizes the casting of one's sins into a body of water.

b. Day of Atonement: The Ten Days of Penitence begin with the New Year and last until the Day of Atonement (Yom Kippur). This is considered the most solemn time of the year when all are judged and their fate determined for the coming year. On Yom Kippur it is the tradition to fast from sunset until nightfall the following day. In the synagogue special prayers for forgiveness are recited. At the end of the service the shofar is sounded.

Moral Failure

In the Yom Kippur service, moral failure is confessed:

We have sinned against you through bribery. And we have sinned against you through slander. We have sinned against you through gluttony. And we have sinned against you through wanton glances. We have sinned against you by rashly judging others. And we have sinned against you through selfishness. We have sinned against you through stubbornness. And we have sinned against you through gossip. We have sinned against you through baseless hatred. And we have sinned against you by succumbing to dismay.

For all these sins, forgiving God, forgive us, pardon us and grant us atonement.[11]

---

6. Days of Joy: In the Jewish calendar there are a number of joyous festivals on which Jews are permitted to follow their daily tasks:

a. Hanukkah: This festival is celebrated for eight days beginning on 25 Kislev – it commemorates the victory of the Maccabees over the Seleucids in the second century CE. The central observance of this festival is the kindling of the festive lamp (menorah) on each of the eight days.

b. Purim: This festival is celebrated on the 14th of Adar to commemorate the deliverance of Persian Jewry from the plans of Haman, the chief minister of King Ahasuerus. In most congregations Purim resembles a carnival – children frequently attend the reading from the scroll of Esther in fancy dress, and whenever Haman's name is mentioned, worshippers stamp their feet and whirl noisemakers (greggers).

c. Rosh Hodesh: This festival of joy occurs with the New Moon each month. There is a special liturgy that celebrates this festive occasion.

d. Tu Bi-Shevat: This joyous festival is the New Year for Trees which takes place on the 15th of Shevat. Among the fruits eaten on Tu Bi-Shevat were those of the Holy Land. In Israel new trees are planted during this festival.

e. Israel Independence Day: This is Israel's national day, which commemorates the proclamation of its independence on the 5th of Iyyar, 1948. The Chief Rabbinate of Israel declared it a religious holiday and established a special order of service for evening and morning worship.

Hanukkah

On each of the eight nights of Hanukkah candles are lit, one the first night, two the second, adding one candle each subsequent night:

Praised are you, Lord our God, king of the universe whose mitzvot (commandments) add holiness to our life and who gave us the mitzvah to light the lights of Hanukkah.
    Praised are you, Lord our God, king of the universe who accomplished miracles for our ancestors in ancient days and in our time ...
    Rock of Ages, let our song praise your saving power. You amid the raging throng were our sheltering tower. Furious they assailed us, but your help availed us. And your word broke their sword when our own strength failed us.[12]

---

7. Life-cycle Events: In Scripture the first commandment is to be fruitful and multiply (Genesis 1:28). In biblical times childbirth took place in a kneeling position or sitting on a special birthstool. Scriptural law imposes various laws on ritual purity and impurity on the mother. In ancient times the birth of a child was accompanied by numerous superstitious practices, including the use of amulets to ward off the evil eye. The naming of a newborn child takes place on one of two occasions: a baby boy is named at the circumcision ceremony; a baby girl is named in the synagogue. The custom of redeeming first-born male children is based on the biblical prescription that first-born sons should be consecrated to the Temple.

According to Jewish law, all male children are to undergo circumcision as a sign of the covenant between God and Abraham's offspring. Jewish ritual circumcision involves the removal of the entire foreskin. It is to be performed on the eighth day after the birth of the child by a person who is properly qualified (mohel). At 13 a boy attains the age of Jewish adulthood. From this point, he is accounted as part of the quorum for prayer (minyan). The bar mitzvah ceremony involves prayer with tefillin (phylacteries) for the first time, and reading from the Torah. Unlike bar mitzvah there is no legal requirement for a girl to take part in a religious ceremony to mark her religious majority (at the age of 12). However, in modern times the practice of bat mitzvah for girls has become commonplace.

Bar Mitzvah

The following prayer is for a bar mitzvah:

May He who blessed our ancestors, Abraham, Isaac and Jacob, bless this youth who was called up today in honour of God and in honour of the Torah, and to give thanks for all the good that God has done for him. As a reward for this, may the Holy One, praised be He, keep him and grant him life. May He incline his heart to be perfect with him, to study his law, to walk in his ways, to observe his commandments, statutes and judgements. May he be successful and prosperous in all his ways, and may he find grace and mercy in the eyes of God and man. May his parents deserve to raise him up to the study of the Law, to the nuptial canopy and to good deeds.[13]

---

8. Marriage: According to tradition, marriage is God's plan for humanity, as illustrated in the story of Adam and Eve in the Book of Genesis. In the Jewish faith it is viewed as a sacred bond as well as a means to personal fulfilment. It is more than a legal contract; rather an institution with cosmic significance, legitimized through divine authority. The purpose of marriage is to build a home, create a family and thereby perpetuate society. In modern times the traditional wedding ceremony normally follows a uniform pattern. The ceremony itself can be held anywhere, but typically it takes place in the synagogue or the synagogue courtyard.

In a traditional ceremony the groom signs the ketubah (marriage contract). He is led to the bride and covers her face with a veil. The couple are then led to the marriage canopy (huppah), accompanied by their parents. According to custom those leading the couple carry lighted candles. When the participants are under the canopy the rabbi recites the blessing over wine and other blessings. Then the bride and groom drink from the cup. The groom then recites the traditional formula: 'Behold you are consecrated unto me with this ring according to the law of Moses and of Israel.' He then puts the ring on the bride's right index finger. To demonstrate that the act of marriage consists of two ceremonies, the ketubah is read. The seven blessings are then recited over a second cup of wine. The ceremony concludes with the groom stepping on a glass and breaking it.

Wedding Ceremony

After the rabbi takes his place under the canopy, the bridegroom is led by his father and mother to the huppah. The rabbi then says:

May he who cometh be blessed.
He who is supremely mighty; He who is supremely praised; He who is supremely great; May He bless this bridegroom and bride.

After the bride is led by her parents to the huppah, the rabbi says:

May she who cometh be blessed.
Mighty is our God. Auspicious signs, and good fortune. Praiseworthy is the bridegroom. Praiseworthy and handsome is the bride.

The rabbi then fills a goblet of wine and recites two benedictions:

Praised be Thou, O Lord our God, king of the universe, who has created the fruit of the vine.
Praised be Thou, O Lord our God, king of the universe, who has sanctified us with thy commandments, and hast commanded us concerning forbidden connections, and hast forbidden us those who are merely betrothed, but hast allowed to us those lawfully married to us through huppah and betrothal. Praised be Thou, O Lord our God, who sanctifiest Thy people Israel through huppah and betrothal.[14]

---

9. Mikveh (Ritual Bath); Leviticus 11:36 specifies that a purification ritual should take place after ritual impurity for individuals and utensils:

'Only a spring, cistern, or collection (mikveh) shall be cleansing.' In Temple times this was applied to a variety of causes of ritual impurity. Later, it was applied primarily to women after menstruation. It is emphasized that the purpose of immersion is not physical but spiritual cleanliness. According to tradition, husbands and wives may not have sexual relations during the days of the wife's monthly period, nor for seven clear days afterwards. This means that among the Orthodox the wedding date is calculated to fit in with the bride's menstrual flow so that she is married during her 'clean period'. During the time that she is forbidden to her husband, the couple sleep in separate beds and avoid touching each other in any way. Then, after the flow has ended and seven full days have elapsed, the wife visits the ritual bath. For immersion to be valid, every inch of the surface of a woman's body must come into contact with the ritual water so that all trace of dirt be removed. Finger and toe nails are trimmed and the hair is thoroughly combed out. Among the Strictly Orthodox, it is the practice for married women to cut off their hair and wear a wig. This has the double benefit of fulfilling the commandment that married women must cover their hair and it makes the monthly visit to the ritual bath easier to manage. When the supervisor is satisfied that the woman is completely clean and her hair free from tangles, she is directed to the ritual bath itself. There she immerses completely so that the waters cover her head, and she recites the traditional blessings. Then she can resume marital relations with her husband.

Mikveh Monologues

One woman gave an account of her own recent and unexpected experience of mikveh following a major life-changing operation, and of the almost mystical synchronicity of events which brought it about. This had led her to consider the new wider usage of mikveh as a powerful and positive experience on an individual level, beyond fertility and reproduction into all kinds of life-cycle events, with its associated concept of rebirth and renewal through water …

Several women expressed a desire to see a new mikveh ritual instituted for other key events in their lives. One said, 'I have a vision of a cross-communal mikveh', and another told us of women's centres in Israel where a particular point is made of asking the mikveh attendants to look out for signs of domestic violence injuries on women who use the mikveh. Another suggestion was that since mikveh is getting very positive responses from feminists who were

> once very critical about the practice, it would be an appropriate area
> for the Jewish Women's Network to take a lead.[15]

10. Home: In Judaism, religious observance in the home is of fundamental importance. Like in the synagogue, such observance continues
various traditions of the ancient Temple. The Sabbath candles, for example,
recall the Temple menorah, and the dining table symbolizes the altar.
Most significantly, within the home, family life is sanctified. As head of the
family, the father is to exercise authority over his wife and children. He is
obligated to circumcise his son, redeem him if he is the first-born, teach
him Torah, marry him off and teach him a craft. Further, he is required to
serve as a role model for the transmission of Jewish ideals to his offspring.
Regarding women, the prevailing sentiment is that the role of the wife is
to bear children and exercise responsibility for family life. Children are
expected to carry out the commandment to honour and respect their
parents.

Symbols of the Jewish religion characterize the Jewish home, beginning
with the mezuzah on each doorpost. In Scripture it is written that 'these
words' shall be written on the doorposts (mezuzot) of the house. This
prescription is understood literally: two passages from Scripture
(Deuteronomy 6:4–9; 11:13–21) are copied by hand on a piece of
parchment, put into a case, and affixed to the doorpost of every room in
the house. At the beginning of the Sabbath the kiddush prayer is recited
over wine prior to the evening meal. Before meals on the Sabbath as well
as on ordinary days, a blessing over food is recited. After the meal, a Grace
after Meals is said.

The cycle of the year provides various opportunities for home observances. During Passover, normal dishes are replaced. The seder itself is
observed in the home; during the service the Haggadah prayer book is read,
and a special seder dish is prepared which includes various symbolic foods
commemorating the Exodus from Egypt. During Sukkot it is customary,
as mentioned, to eat and dwell in a temporary structure (sukkah) built for
the festival. During Hanukkah a festival lamp (menorah) is kindled at home
on each day of the festival. Life-cycle events also provide an occasion for
special observances in the home, including circumcision. At the time of
mourning, friends and visitors come to the home during the seven days of
mourning (shivah), where a quorum (minyan) recites prayers.

11. Dietary Laws: According to the Jewish tradition, food must be
ritually fit (kosher) if it is to be eaten. The Bible declares that the laws of
kashrut (dietary laws) were given by God to Moses on Mount Sinai. Thus

Jews are obligated to follow this legislation because of its divine origin. The laws concerning which animals, birds and fish may be eaten are contained in Leviticus 11 and Deuteronomy 14:3–21. Scripture specifies that only those animals that both chew the cud and have split hooves may be eaten. No similar formula is given concerning which birds may be consumed; rather a list is given of forbidden birds such as the eagle, the owl and the raven. Regarding fish, the law states that only fish that have both fins and scales are allowed. A further category of kashrut deals with the method of killing animals for food (shehitah). The act of slaughter must be done with a sharpened knife without a single notch, since that might tear the animal's food- or wind-pipe. Another restriction concerning ritual food is the prohibition against eating milk and meat together.

12. Death and Mourning: Concerning death the Bible declares that human beings will return to the dust of the earth (Genesis 3:19). The rabbis of the Talmud declared that death occurs when respiration has stopped. Jewish law stipulates that no effort should be spared to save a dying patient. Yet despite such an attitude, traditional Judaism fosters an acceptance of death when it is inevitable. Once death has been determined, the eyes and mouth are closed. The body is then put on the floor, covered with a sheet, and a lighted candle is placed close to the head. Mirrors are covered in the home of the deceased, and any standing water is poured out. A dead body is not to be left unattended. The burial of the body should take place as soon as possible. After the members of the burial society have taken care of the body, they prepare it for burial. It is washed and dressed in a white linen shroud. The corpse is then placed in a coffin or on a bier before the funeral service. Traditional Jews only permit the use of a plain wooden coffin. The deceased is then borne to the grave. A marker should be placed on a newly filled grave, and a tombstone should be erected and unveiled as soon as permissible.

Judaism provides a special framework for mourning. The mourning period, known as shivah (seven), lasts for seven days beginning with the day of burial. During this time mourners sit on the floor or on low cushions or benches and are forbidden to shave, bathe, go to work, study the Torah, engage in sexual relations, wear leather shoes, greet others, cut their hair, or wear laundered clothing. Through these seven days, it is customary to visit mourners. Shivah concludes on the morning of the seventh day and is followed by mourning of a lesser intensity for thirty days known as sheloshim (thirty).

Chapter 2

The Enlightenment and Modern Jewish Life

The Hebrew Bible traces the history of the Jewish people from its origins until the Hellenistic period. In subsequent centuries rabbinic Judaism became normative and continued until the early Middle Ages. Through this long period Jews remained faithful to the traditions of their ancestors and Jewish life was regulated by the fundamental beliefs and practices outlined in Chapter 1. During the Middle Ages, Jewish learning continued to flourish and major contributions were made to the development of the legal, philosophical and mystical traditions. In many respects the medieval period extended into the eighteenth century for the Jewish community. Despite the numerous changes taking place in European society, monarchs continued to rule by divine right. In addition, the aristocracy was exempt from taxation and enjoyed special privileges; the established Church retained control over religious matters; and merchants and artisans closed ranks against outsiders. At the other end of the social scale peasants continued to be burdened with obligations to feudal masters, and in eastern and central Europe serfs were enslaved and exploited. By 1770 nearly two million Jews lived in this environment in Christian Europe. In some countries such as England and Holland they were relatively free from economic and social restrictions. The English and Dutch governments, for example, did not interfere with the private affairs and religious life of the Jewish population. Central European Jewry, however, was subject to a wide range of oppressive legal restrictions, and Jews were confined to special areas of residence. Furthermore, Jews were forced to sew signs on their cloaks or wear special hats to distinguish them from their non-Jewish neighbours.

Jewish Emancipation

By the 1770s and 1780s the treatment of Jews in central Europe greatly improved due to the influence of such polemicists as Wilhelm Christian Dohm. In an influential tract, *Concerning the Amelioration of the Civil Status of the Jews*, Dohm argued that Jews did not pose any threat and could become valuable and patriotic citizens. A wise and benevolent society, he argued, should abolish restrictions that prevent the Jewish population from having close contact with Christians and acquiring secular knowledge. All occupations, he argued, should be open to Jews and educational opportunities should be provided.

The Holy Roman Emperor Joseph II echoed such sentiments. In 1781 he abolished the Jewish badge as well as taxes imposed on Jewish travellers. In the following year he issued an edict of toleration that granted Jews of Vienna freedom in trade and industry and the right of residence outside Jewish quarters. Moreover, regulations prohibiting Jews from leaving their homes before noon on Sunday and attending places of public amusement were abolished. Jews were also permitted to send their children to state schools or set up their own educational institutions. In 1784 Jewish judicial autonomy was abolished and three years later some Jews were inducted into the Hapsburg army.

Edict of Toleration

The Holy Roman Emperor Joseph II issued an edict of toleration in 1781:

> In order to make the Jews more useful, discriminatory Jewish clothing which has been worn in the past is now abolished. Within two years the Jews must abandon their own language: from now on all their contracts, bonds, wills, accounts, ledgers, certificates and any legally binding document must be drawn up in German ... Jews may continue to use their own language during religious services ... Jews who do not have the opportunity of sending children to Jewish schools must send them to Christian ones to learn reading, writing, arithmetic and other subjects ... Jews will also be permitted to attend the imperial universities ... Leaders of local communities must rationally instruct their people that the Jews may be treated like any other fellow human being. There must be an end to the prejudice and

> contempt which some subjects, particularly the less intelligent,
> have shown towards the Jewish people.[1]

As in Germany, reforms in France during the 1770s and 1780s ameliorated the situation of the Jewish population. Though Sephardic Jews in Paris and the south and southwest lived in comfort and security, the Ashkenazic Jews of Alsace and Lorraine had a traditional Jewish lifestyle and were subject to a variety of disabilities. In 1789 the National Assembly issued a declaration proclaiming that all human beings are born and remain free and equal in rights and that no person should be persecuted for his opinions as long as they do not subvert civil law. In 1790 the Sephardim of southwest France and Jews from Papal Avignon were granted citizenship. This decree was followed in September 1791 by a resolution that granted citizenship rights to all Jews. This change in Jewish status occurred elsewhere in Europe as well – in 1796 the Dutch Jews of the Batavian republic were also granted full citizenship rights and in 1797 the ghettos of Padua and Rome were abolished.

In 1799 Napoleon became the First Consul of France and five years later he was proclaimed emperor. Napoleon's Code of Civil Law propounded in 1804 established the right of all inhabitants to follow any trade and declared equality for all. After 1806 a number of German principalities were united in the French kingdom of Westphalia, where Jews were granted the same rights. Despite these advances the situation of Jews did not undergo a complete transformation, and Napoleon still desired to regulate Jewish affairs. In July 1806 he convened an Assembly of Jewish Notables to consider a number of issues. Do Jewish marriage and divorce procedures conflict with French civil law? Are Jews allowed to marry Christians? Do French Jews consider Frenchmen their compatriots and is France their country?

In reply, the Assembly decreed that Jewish law is compatible with French civil law; Jewish divorce and marriage are not binding unless preceded by civil law; mixed marriage is legal but cannot be sanctioned by the Jewish faith; France is the homeland of French Jews and Frenchmen should be seen as their kin. In the next year, Napoleon summoned a Grand Sanhedrin consisting of rabbis and laymen to confirm the views of the Assembly. This body pledged its allegiance to the emperor and nullified any features of the Jewish tradition that conflicted with the requirements of citizenship. In 1808 Napoleon issued two edicts regarding the Jewish community. In the first he set up a system of district boards of rabbis and laymen (consistories) to regulate Jewish affairs under the supervision of a central body from Paris. These consistories were responsible for maintaining synagogues and religious institutions, enforcing laws of conscription, overseeing changes in occupations ordered by the government and acting as a local police force. Napoleon's second decree postponed, reduced or abrogated all debts owed to Jews, regulated Jewish trade and residence rights and prohibited Jewish army conscripts from hiring substitutes.

Napoleon's Sanhedrin

As a result of the Assembly of Notables, Napoleon revived the institution of the Sanhedrin. Not all reactions were favourable. In 1807 the Holy Synod of the Russian Orthodox Church ordered the following proclamation to be read in all the churches:

> In order to complete the degradation of the Church, [Napoleon] has convened the Jewish synagogues of France, restored the dignity of the rabbis and laid the foundation of a new Hebrew Sanhedrin, the same notorious tribunal which dared to condemn Our Lord and Saviour Jesus Christ to the cross. He now has the audacity to gather together all of the Jews whom God, in his anger, had scattered over the face of the earth, and launch all of them into the destruction of Christ's Church.[2]

The French Revolution of 1848, which led to outbreaks of revolt in Prussia, Austria, Hungary, Italy and Bohemia, forced rulers to grant constitutions that guaranteed freedom of speech, assembly and religion. In Germany a National Assembly was convened to draft a constitution that included a bill of rights designating civil, political and religious liberty for all Germans. Although this constitution did not come into effect, because the revolt was suppressed, the 1850s and 1860s witnessed economic and industrial expansion in Germany in which liberal politicians advocated a policy of civil equality. In 1869 the parliament of the North German Federation proclaimed Jewish emancipation for all its constituents, and by 1871, when all of Germany excluding Austria became the German Reich under the Hohenzollern dynasty, Jewish emancipation was complete: all restrictions concerning professions, marriage, real estate and the right to vote were eliminated.

Jewish Life in Eastern Europe

Compared with the West, the social and political conditions of eastern European Jewry were less conducive to emancipation. After the partitions of Poland in the latter half of the eighteenth century and the decision of the Congress of Vienna to place the Duchy of Warsaw under Alexander I, most of Polish Jewry was under Russian rule. At the beginning of the nineteenth century, Russia preserved its previous social order: social classes were legally segregated; the aristocracy maintained its privileges; the peasantry lived as serfs; and the Church was under state control. In many towns and villages during this period Jews were in the majority and engaged in a wide range of occupations. In the countryside they worked as leasers of estates, mills, forests, distilleries and inns, but increasingly many of these village Jews migrated to larger urban centres where they became part of the working class. Despite this influx to the cities, the Jewish population retained its traditional religious and ethnic distinctiveness.

Initially, Catherine the Great exhibited tolerance towards her Jewish subjects. But in 1791 Jewish merchants were prohibited from settling in central Russia. Only in the southern Ukraine were Jews allowed to establish a community. This exception was followed several years later by the granting of permission for Jews to live in other areas, such as Kiev. In 1804 Alexander II specified territory in western Russia as an area in which Jews would be allowed to reside – this was known as the Pale of Settlement. After several attempts to expel Jews from the countryside, the tsar in 1817 initiated a new policy of integrating the Jewish community into the population by founding a society of Israelite Christians, which extended legal and financial concessions to baptized Jews.

Pale of Settlement

The Pale of Settlement included 15 provinces in Western Russia and 10 provinces of the former Kingdom of Poland:

A permanent residence is permitted to the Jews: (a) in the provinces: Grodno, Vilna, Volhynia, Podolia, Minsk, Ekaterinoslav; (b) in the districts: Bessarabia, Bialystok. Jews who have gone abroad without a legal exist permit are deprived of Russian citizenship and not permitted to return to Russia. Within the general area of settlement and in every place where the Jews are permitted permanent residence, they are allowed not only to move from place to place and to settle in accordance with the general regulations, but also to acquire real estate of all kinds, with the exception of inhabited estates, the ownership of which is strictly forbidden to Jews.[3]

In 1824 the deportation of Jews from villages began; in the same year Alexander I died and was succeeded by Nicholas I, who adopted a severe attitude to the Jewish community. In 1827 he implemented a policy of inducting Jewish boys into the Russian army for a 25-year period in order to increase the number of converts to Christianity. Nicholas I also deported Jews from villages in certain areas. In 1827 they were expelled from Kiev and three years later from the surrounding province. In 1835 the Russian government propagated a revised code of laws to regulate Jewish settlement in the western border. In order to reduce Jewish isolation, the government set out to reform education in 1841; a young Jewish educator, Max Lilienthal, was asked to establish in the Pale of Settlement a number of reformed Jewish schools, which incorporated Western educational methods. Initially, Lilienthal sought to persuade Jewish leaders that by supporting this project the Jewish community could improve their lot, but when he discovered that the intention of the tsar was to undermine the Talmud he left the country. These new schools were created in 1844 but attracted only small numbers, and the Russian government eventually abandoned its plans.

In the same year Nicholas I abolished the kehillot (Jewish communities) and put Jewry under the authority of the police as well as municipal government. Yet despite this policy it was impossible for the Russian administration to carry out the functions of the kehillot, and it was recognized that a Jewish body was needed to recruit students for state military schools and to collect taxes. Between 1850–1 the government attempted to forbid Jewish dress, men's side-curls, and the ritual of shaving women's hair. In 1851 a plan was initiated to categorize all Jews along economic lines: those who were considered useful subjects included craftsmen, farmers, and wealthy merchants, whereas the vast majority of Jews were liable to further restrictions. After the Crimean War of 1853–6, Alexander II emancipated the serfs, modernized the judiciary and established a system of local self-government. In addition, he allowed certain groups, including wealthy merchants, university graduates, certified artisans, discharged soldiers and all holders of diplomas, to reside outside the Pale of Settlement. As a result, Jewish communities appeared in St Petersburg and Moscow. Furthermore, a limited number of Jews were allowed to enter the legal profession and participate in district councils. Government-sponsored schools also attracted more Jewish students, and in the 1860s and 1870s emancipated Jews began to take an active role in the professions and in Russian economic life.

The Jewish Enlightenment

These changes in the status of Jewry heralded the transformation of Jewish existence in the modern world. The father of the Jewish enlightenment was the eighteenth-century Jewish philosopher, Moses Mendelssohn. Born in Dessau, Mendelssohn travelled to Berlin as a young student, where he pursued secular as well as religious studies and befriended leading figures of the German Enlightenment, such as Gotthold Ephraim Lessing. Under Lessing's influence, Mendelssohn published a number of theological studies in which he argued for the existence of God and creation, and propounded the view that human reason is able to discover the reality of God, divine providence and the immortality of the soul.

When challenged by a Christian apologist to explain why he remained loyal to the Jewish faith, Mendelssohn published – in 1783 – a defence of the Jewish religion: *Jerusalem, or On Religious Power and Judaism*. In this study Mendelssohn contended that no religious institution should use coercion. Neither the Church nor the state, he believed, has the right to impose its religious views on the individual. Addressing the question as to whether the Mosaic law sanctions such coercion, Mendelssohn stressed that Judaism does not coerce the mind through dogma. With regard to the Jews, he wrote: 'The Israelites possess a Divine legislation – laws, commandments, statutes, rules of conduct and instruction in God's will and in what they are to do to attain temporal and eternal salvation. Moses, in a miraculous and supernatural way, revealed to them these laws and commandments, but not dogmas.' The purpose of this legal code, Mendelssohn argued, was to make Israel into a priest people.

For Mendelssohn Jewish law does not give power to the authorities to persecute individuals for holding false doctrines. Yet Jews, he argued, should not absolve themselves from following God's law: 'Adopt the mores and constitution of the country in which you find yourself,' he declared, 'but be steadfast in upholding the religion of your fathers, too.' Thus, despite Mendelssohn's recognition of the common links between Judaism and other faiths, he followed the traditions of his ancestors and advocated the retention of the distinctive features of the Jewish faith. By combining philosophical theism and Jewish traditionalism, Mendelssohn attempted to transcend the constrictions of ghetto life and enter the mainstream of Western European culture as an observant Jew.

To bring about the modernization of Jewish life, Mendelssohn also translated the Pentateuch into German so that Jews would be able to learn the language of the country in which they lived, and he spearheaded a commentary on Scripture (*Biur*) which combined Jewish scholarship with secular thought. Following Mendelssohn's example, a number of Prussian followers known as the maskilim fostered a Jewish Enlightenment – the Haskalah – which encouraged Jews to abandon medieval patterns of life and thought. The maskilim also attempted to reform Jewish education by widening the curriculum to include secular subjects. To further this end, they wrote textbooks in Hebrew and established Jewish schools. The maskilim also produced the first Jewish literary magazine, *The Gatherer*, in 1783. Contributors to this publication wrote poems and fables in the classical style of biblical Hebrew and produced studies of biblical exegesis, Hebrew linguistics and Jewish history.

By the 1820s the centre of this movement had shifted to the Austrian Empire. A new journal, *First Fruits of the Times*, was published in Vienna between 1821 and 1832 and was followed between 1833 and 1856 by a Hebrew journal, *Vineyard of Delight*, devoted to modern Jewish scholarship. In the 1840s the Haskalah spread to Russia, where writers made important contributions to Hebrew literature and translated textbooks and European fiction into Hebrew. During the reign of Alexander II, Hebrew weeklies appeared and the Society for the Promotion of Culture among Jews of Russia was established in 1863. In the next two decades maskilim produced works of social and literary criticism. These thinkers, however, were not typical of the Jewish masses. Many lived isolated lives because of their support of the Austrian and Russian governments' efforts to reform Jewish life. In addition, they were violently critical of traditional rabbinic Judaism and so were regarded with suspicion and hostility.

The Reform of Judaism

At the beginning of the nineteenth century the Jewish financier and communal leader Israel Jacobson initiated a programme of reform. He founded a boarding school for boys in Sessen, Westphalia in 1801, and subsequently established other schools throughout the kingdom. In these new foundations general subjects were taught by Christian teachers, while a Jewish instructor gave lessons about Judaism. The consistory under Jacobson's leadership also introduced external reforms to the Jewish worship service, including choral hymns and addresses, and prayers in German. In 1810 Jacobson built the first Reform temple next to the school, which was dedicated in the presence of Christian clergy and dignitaries. After Napoleon's defeat, Jacobson moved to Berlin, where he attempted to put these principles into practice by founding the Berlin temple. In Hamburg in 1817 a Reform temple was opened in which a number of innovations were made to the liturgy, including prayers and sermons in German as well as choral singing and organ music. To defend these alterations Hamburg reformers cited the Talmud in support of their actions.

Hamburg Reform Temple

In 1818 the Hamburg Reform Temple issued its own prayer book. The Constitution of the Temple sought to justify these changes:

Public worship has for some time been neglected by too many because there is less and less knowledge of the language in which it is traditionally conducted and also because many other corruptions have crept in over the years. Because of this, the undersigned, convinced of the necessity of restoring pubic worship to its proper place and dignity, have combined to follow the example of several Israelitish congregations, particularly in Berlin.[4]

The central aim of these early reformers was to adapt Jewish worship to contemporary aesthetic standards. For these innovators the informality of the traditional service seemed foreign and undignified, and they therefore insisted on greater decorum, more unison in prayer, a choir, hymns and musical responses as well as alterations in prayer and the length of the service. Paralleling this development, other Jews sought to encourage the systematic study of Jewish history and founded the Society for the Culture and Academic Study of Judaism. The purpose of this new approach to the past was to gain a true understanding of the origins of the Jewish tradition in the history of Western civilization.

In response to these developments, Orthodox Jews asserted that any alteration to the tradition was a violation of the Jewish heritage. For these traditionalists the written and oral Torah constituted an infallible chain of divinely revealed truth. The most prominent of these scholars was

Samson Raphael Hirsch, the Chief Rabbi of the Duchy of Oldenburg. In 1836 he published the *Nineteen Letters on Judaism*, a defence of Orthodoxy in the form of essays by a young rabbi to a friend who questioned the importance of remaining a Jew. In Hirsch's view the purpose of human life is not to attain personal happiness and perfection; rather, humans should strive to serve God by obeying his will. To serve as an example of such devotion, the Jewish nation was formed so that through its way of life all people would come to know that true happiness lies in obeying God. Thus the people of Israel were given the Promised Land in order to be able to keep God's law. When the Jewish nation was exiled, they were able to fulfil this mission by remaining loyal to God and to the Torah despite constant persecution.

Samson Raphael Hirsch

The most eloquent critic of Reform Judaism was Samson Raphael Hirsch, the founder of Neo-Orthodoxy in the middle of the nineteenth century:

> It was not the 'Orthodox' Jews who introduced the word 'orthodoxy' into the Jewish discussion. It was the modern 'progressive' Jews who first applied this name to 'old', 'backward' Jews as a derogatory term. This name was at first resented by 'old' Jews. And rightly so. 'Orthodox' Judaism does not know any varieties of Judaism. It conceives Judaism as one and indivisible. It does not know a Mosaic, prophetic and rabbinic Judaism, nor Orthodox and Liberal Judaism. It knows only Judaism and non-Judaism.[5]

Despite Hirsch's criticisms, a number of German rabbis who had been influenced by the Enlightenment began to re-evaluate the Jewish tradition. In this undertaking the achievements of Jewish scholars who engaged in the scientific study of Judaism had a profound influence. In the early half of the nineteenth century, Reform spread to other countries such as England. But it was in Frankfurt that Reform Judaism became most radical. In 1842 the Society of the Friends of Reform was founded and published a proclamation justifying their innovative approach to tradition. A similar group, the Association for the Reform of Judaism, was founded in Berlin in 1844 under the leadership of Samuel Holdheim. In the same year the first Reform synod took place in Brunswick in which the participants advocated the formulation of a Jewish creed and the modification of Sabbath and dietary laws as well as the traditional liturgy. This consultation was followed the next year by a meeting in Frankfurt which recommended that petitions for the return to Israel and the restoration of the Jewish state be omitted from the prayer book. At this meeting one of the more conservative rabbis, Zecharias Frankel, expressed his dissatisfaction with the decision of the synod to regard the use of Hebrew in worship as advisable rather than necessary and resigned from the Assembly. Subsequently, he became head of a Jewish theological seminary in Breslau, which was based on free enquiry combined with a commitment to the Jewish tradition. The revolution of 1848 and its aftermath brought about the cessation of these conferences, and nearly a generation passed before reformers met again to formulate a common policy.

In the United States, Reform Judaism took root and flourished during this period. Prominent among these early reformers was a Bohemian-born rabbi, Isaac Mayer Wise, who published a new Reform prayer book, *Minhag Amerika*, and in 1869 established the Central Conference of American Reform Rabbis, and four years later the Union of American Hebrew Congregations. In 1875 he also founded the Hebrew Union College, the first Reform seminary on American soil. But the principles of American Reform Judaism were not explicitly set out until 1885 when a gathering of Reform rabbis met in Pittsburgh. Their deliberations resulted in the adoption of a formal list of principles, the Pittsburgh Platform. In his address to the conference, the chairman, Kaufmann Kohler, stated that their purpose was to show that Judaism must be modernized in order to embrace the findings of scientific research as well as the fields of comparative religion and biblical criticism. The Platform itself began with the statement that Judaism presents the highest conception of God. In this connection the conference spoke of the Bible as the most potent instrument of religious and moral instruction; for these reformers Scripture was also seen as compatible with the findings of science. The participants further decreed that they recognized only the moral commandments as well as those rituals that they viewed as spiritually uplifting. Laws regulating diet, priestly purity and dress were rejected as anachronistic. The belief in a personal Messiah was eliminated and replaced by a messianic hope for the establishment of a kingdom of justice and peace for humanity. The reformers also asserted that Judaism is a progressive religion ever striving to be in accord with the postulates of reason. Regarding the afterlife, the participants subscribed to the belief in the immortality of the soul rather than the traditional doctrines of bodily resurrection and reward and punishment in the hereafter. As a conclusion to their document, the delegates proclaimed their commitment to engage in social action.

Pittsburgh Platform

The principles of Reform Judaism in the United States were established at the Pittsburgh Conference in 1885:

We hold that Judaism presents the highest conception of the God-idea as taught in our holy Scriptures and developed and spiritualized by the Jewish teachers in accordance with the moral and philosophical progress of their respective ages …

We hold that the modern discoveries of scientific researches in the domains of nature and history are not antagonistic to the doctrines of Judaism …

Today we accept as binding only the moral laws and maintain only such ceremonies as elevate and sanctify our lives, but reject all such as are not adapted to the views and habits of modern civilization …

We hold that all such Mosaic and rabbinical laws as regulate diet, priestly purity and dress originated in ages and under the influence of ideas altogether foreign to our present mental and spiritual state …

We consider ourselves no longer a nation but a religious community, and therefore expect neither a return to Palestine, nor a sacrificial worship under the administration of the sons of Aaron …

We recognize in Judaism a progressive religion, ever striving to be in accord with the postulates of reason …

We reassert the doctrines of Judaism that the soul of man is immortal … we reject as ideas not rooted in Judaism the belief both in bodily resurrection and Gehenna (Hell) and Eden, as abodes for everlasting punishment and reward …

In full accord with the spirit of Mosaic legislation … we deem it our duty to participate in the great task of modern times, to solve on the basis of justice and righteousness the problems presented by the contrasts and evils of the present organization of society.[6]

The Rise of Anti-Semitism

By the last decades of the nineteenth century, the European Jewish community had attained a high degree of emancipation. Nevertheless, political conditions in Europe after 1870 had brought about considerable disruption. Several proud and independent nations had emerged and fought against indigenous minority groups that threatened their homogeneity. In such places, Jews were viewed as aliens and inassimilable. Symptomatic of such attitudes was the invention of the term anti-Semitism by the German journalist Wilhelm Marr in 1870. Previously, Jewish persecution was based largely on religious grounds but Marr's concept of anti-Semitism focused on biological descent. Anti-Semitism was thus a racist policy, which significantly differed from previous dislike of Jews and Judaism. For Marr the Jews had corrupted all standards, banned all idealism from society, dominated commerce, and pushed themselves ever more in state services. In addition, they ruled the theatre and formed a social political phalanx. According to Marr, there is a continuous struggle in contemporary society between these Semitic aliens and native Teutonic stock.

Wilhelm Marr

Wilhelm Marr was a racial anti-Semite whose pamphlet, *The Victory of Judaism over Germandom: Regarded from a Non-Denominational Point of View*, compared the Jew with the German:

> Jewry's control of society and politics, as well its practical domination of religious and ecclesiastical thought, is still in the prime of development ...
>
> By now, a sudden reversal of this process is fundamentally impossible, for if it were, the entire social structure, which has been thoroughly Judaized, would collapse, and there is no viable alternative to this social structure which could take its place ... We were vanquished and it is entirely proper that the victor shouts 'Vae Victis!'
>
> German culture has proved itself ineffective and powerless against this foreign power ... The Jews were late in their assault against Germany, but once they started there was no stopping them.[7]

Anti-Jewish feelings intensified in the 1870s in Germany as a result of economic and cultural upheaval. The political liberalism of previous decades had enabled Jews to benefit from economic activities, and in reaction conservatives blamed the Jewish community for the ills of society. Antipathy towards Jews in France was exploited by the monarchy and clergy to counter the liberal ideas of the French Revolution. Such anti-Semitism reached a climax with the Dreyfus affair. Accused of treason, Alfred Dreyfus was banished from the army and sentenced to life imprisonment. Later, however, it was discovered that forged evidence had been used to implicate Dreyfus and a scandal ensued that divided public opinion. In Russia anti-Semitism became an official policy of the state. After Alexander II was assassinated in 1881, a succession of pogroms against the Jewish population took place in southern Ukraine.

Such manifestations of anti-Jewish sentiment were based on the belief that the Jewish people constitute a dangerous racial group. Ideologues argued that the Semitic mentality was egoistic, materialistic, economically minded, cowardly and culturally degenerate. In this context a number of writers propagated racist theories. In *The Foundations of the Nineteenth Century*, published at the turn of the century, Houston Stewart Chamberlain maintained that the antiquity and mobility of the Jewish nation illustrates that the confrontation between superior Aryans and parasitic Semites is the central theme of history. Earlier, in the 1880s, the 'Protocols of the Elders of Zion' were believed to be the minutes of a clandestine world government. In this document the elders were depicted as attempting to strengthen their hold over the European economy, the press, and the parties opposed to the tsar as well as other autocratic regimes.

Houston Stewart Chamberlain

British by origin, Houston Stewart Chamberlain espoused racial anti-Semitism in *The Foundations of the Nineteenth Century*:

We live today in a 'Jewish age'; we may think what we like about the past history of the Jews; their present history actually takes up so much room in our own history that we cannot possibly refuse to notice them. Herder in spite of his own outspoken humanism had expressed the opinion that 'the Jewish people is and remains in Europe an Asiatic people alien to our part of the world, bound to that old law which it received in a distant climate, and which according to our own confession, it cannot do away with'. Quite correct. But this alien people, everlastingly alien, because – as Herder well remarks – it is indissolubly bound to an alien law that is hostile to all other peoples – this alien people has become precisely in the course of the nineteenth century a disproportionately important and in many spheres actually dominant constituent of our life. Even a hundred years ago that same witness had sadly to confess that the 'ruder nations of Europe' were 'willingly slaves of Jewish usury'; today he could say the same of by far the greatest part of the civilized world. The possession of money in itself is, however, of least account; our government, our law, our science, our commerce, our literature, our art ... practically all branches of our life have become more or less willing slaves of the Jews.[8]

Zionism

The pogroms of 1881–2 forced many Jews to emigrate; most went to the United States, but a sizeable number were drawn to Palestine. In the Pale of Settlement, nationalist zealots organized Zionist groups (Lovers of Zion) which collected money and organized courses in Hebrew and Jewish history. In 1882 several thousand Jews left for Palestine, where they worked as shopkeepers and artisans. Other Jewish immigrants, known as Bilu (from the Hebrew 'house of Jacob, let us go') combined Marxist ideas with Jewish nationalist fervour and worked as farmers and labourers.

During this period Leon Pinsker, an eminent Russian physician, published *Autoemancipation* in which he argued that the liberation of Jewry could only be secured by the establishment of a Jewish homeland. Nations, he wrote, live side by side in a state of relative peace, which is based chiefly on fundamental equality between them. But it is different with the people of Israel. This people is not counted among the nations, because when it was exiled from its land it lost the essential attributes of nationality by which one nation is distinguished from another.

Leon Pinsker

Leon Pinsker espoused the ideals of the Enlightenment, but after the pogroms of 1881 he became determined to create a Jewish homeland. In 1882 he published *Autoemancipation* in which he argued that the Jewish problem could only be resolved by creating a Jewish commonwealth, since Jews have always been seen as aliens:

> For the living, the Jew is a dead man; for the natives, an alien and a vagrant; for property holders a beggar; for the poor, an exploiter and millionaire; for patriots, a man without a country; for all classes, a hated rival.[9]

In the 1890s the idea of Jewish nationalism had spread to other countries in Europe. Foremost among its proponents was Theodor Herzl, profoundly affected by the Dreyfus affair, who made contact with the Lovers of Zion. In 1897 the first Zionist Congress was held in Basle, calling for a national home for Jews based on international law. At this congress Herzl stated that emancipation of the Jews had been an illusion: Jews were everywhere objects of contempt and hatred. The only solution to the Jewish problem, he argued, was the re-establishment of a Jewish homeland in Palestine. In the same year the Zionist Organization was created, with branches in Europe and America.

After establishing these basic institutions of the Zionist movement, Herzl embarked on diplomatic negotiations. In 1898 he met with Kaiser Wilhelm II, who promised he would take up the matter with the Sultan. When nothing came of this, Herzl attempted to arrange an interview, and in 1901 a meeting was held. In return for a charter of Jewish settlement in Palestine, Herzl suggested that wealthy Jewish bankers might be willing to pay off the Turkish debt. In the following year the Sultan agreed to approve a plan of Jewish settlement throughout the Ottoman Empire, but not a corporate Jewish homeland in Palestine.

Unwilling to abandon a diplomatic approach, Herzl met with Joseph Chamberlain, the British Secretary of State for Colonial Affairs. During their conversation, Chamberlain suggested that El Arish in the Sinai Peninsula might be a feasible area of settlement. Later, Herzl was summoned to London for a second talk with Chamberlain, who explained that he had seen a country which might be suitable: Uganda. At the next

Zionist congress, this plan was discussed. When the resolution to explore this proposal was passed by a small margin, the delegates from Eastern Europe walked out. During the next few days the movement was threatened by schism; at the end of the proceedings the Russian Jews set off for Kharkov, where they convened their own conference committing themselves to the idea of Palestine.

Theodor Herzl

The father of Zionism, Theodor Herzl, was the founder of the World Zionist Organization. In his writing, he argued that the Jewish problem can only be solved by the establishment of a Jewish homeland:

> I am introducing no new idea; on the contrary, it is a very old one. It is a universal idea – and therein lies its power – old as the people, which never even in the time of bitterest calamity ceased to cherish it. This is the restoration of the Jewish state.
>
> It is remarkable that we Jews should have dreamt this kingly dream all through the long night of our history. Now day is dawning. We need only rub the sleep out of our eyes, stretch our limbs, and convert the dream into a reality. Though neither prophet, nor visionary, I confess I cherish the hope and belief that the Jewish people will one day be fired by a splendid enthusiasm …
>
> We have honestly striven everywhere to merge ourselves in the social life of surrounding communities, and to preserve only the faith of our fathers. It has not been permitted to us. In vain are we loyal patriots, in some places, our loyalty running to extremes; in vain do we make the same sacrifices of life and property as our fellow-citizens; in vain do we strive to increase the fame of our native land in science and art, or her wealth by trade and commerce. In countries where we have lived for centuries we are still cried down as strangers; and often by those whose ancestors were not yet domiciled in the land where Jews had already made experience of suffering …
>
> Distress binds us together; and thus united we suddenly discover our strength. Yes, we are strong enough to form a state, and a model state. We possess all human and material resources necessary for the purpose.[10]

In England public opinion was opposed to the transference of Uganda to the Jews and the offer was eventually withdrawn. In the following year, Herzl died and the Zionist movement was led by a new president, David Wolffsohn, who attempted to heal the rifts between competing factions. During the next decade the major developments in the Zionist movement took place in Israel, and by the beginning of the twentieth century a sizeable number of Jews had migrated to Palestine. Most of these pioneers lived in cities but a small minority worked on farm colonies under the control of the Palestine Jewish Colonization Association. In 1904, when a second wave of immigrants departed for the Holy Land, most of these settlers were determined to become farmers.

After the First World War, Jews in Palestine organized a National Assembly and an Executive Council. By the late 1920s Labour Zionism had become a dominant force in Palestinian Jewish life. In 1930 various socialist and Labour groups joined together in the Israel Labour Party. Within the Zionist movement a right-wing segment opposed the President of the Zionist World Congress, Chaim Weizmann, who was committed to cooperating with the British. After several Zionist congresses, the Revisionist movement under Vladimir Jabotinsky formed its own organization.

In 1936 the Arabs, supported by Syria, Iraq and Egypt, commenced an offensive against Jews, the British and moderate Arabs. Eventually, the British government published a White Paper in 1939 which rejected the concept of partition, limited Jewish immigration to 75,000 and decreed that Palestine would become independent in ten years. During the war and afterwards, the British prevented illegal immigrants from entering the Holy Land. In the Jews' struggle against the British, Menachem Begin, the leader of the Revisionist's military arm (the Irgun), played an important role. Finally, the British announced their intention to leave Palestine, and the United Nations was given authority to determine the future of the country. On 29 November 1947 the General Assembly of the United Nations approved the partition of Palestine, and on 14 May 1948 David Ben-Gurion, the Prime Minister of Israel, read out the Scroll of Independence of the Jewish state.

Declaration of the State of Israel

The Scroll of Independence sought to justify the creation of a Jewish homeland in Palestine:

The Land of Israel was the birthplace of the Jewish people.

Here their spiritual, religious and national identity was formed. Here they achieved their independence and created a culture of national and universal significance. Here they wrote and gave their Bible to the world ...

Impelled by this historic association, Jews strove through the centuries to go back to the land of their fathers and regain their Statehood. In recent decades they returned in their masses. They reclaimed the wilderness, revived their language, built cities and villages and established a vigorous and ever-growing community, with its own economic and cultural life ...

In 1897 the First Zionist Congress, inspired by Theodor Herzl's vision of the Jewish State, proclaimed the right of the Jewish people to national revival in their own country.

This right was acknowledged by the Balfour Declaration of 2 November 1917, and reaffirmed by the Mandate of the League of Nations, which gave explicit international recognition to the historic connection of the Jewish people with Palestine and their right to reconstitute their national home ...

On 29 November 1947 the General Assembly of the United Nations adopted a Resolution for the establishment of an independent Jewish State in Palestine, and called upon inhabitants of the country to take such steps as may be necessary on their part to put the plan into effect ...

Accordingly, we, the members of the National Council, representing the Jewish people in Palestine and the Zionist movement of the world, met together in solemn assembly today, the day of the termination of the British Mandate for Palestine, and by virtue of the national and historic right of the Jewish people and of the resolution of the General Assembly of the United Nations, hereby proclaim the establishment of the Jewish State in Palestine, to be called Israel.[11]

Chapter 3

The Holocaust and the State of Israel

Two major interrelated events have profoundly influenced modern Judaism: the tragedy of the Holocaust and the creation of the Jewish state. After its defeat in the First World War, Germany initially flourished as a federal republic. However, the depression of 1930–2 brought about massive unemployment and widespread instability. As a consequence extremist parties gained considerable support, forcing the government to rule by presidential decree. After several unsuccessful conservative coalitions, the president, Field Marshall Paul von Hindenburg, appointed the leader of the National Socialist Worker's Party, Adolf Hitler, as Chancellor. The ideology of the Nazi Party was based on German nationalism, anti-capitalism and anti-Semitism. According to Hitler, the Jews were parasites and degenerates, the treachery of Jewish socialists, liberals and pacifists having cost Germany the war and led to postwar economic and cultural decline. Further, he argued that the Bolshevik revolution was part of a worldwide Jewish plot for world domination. To combat the plans of international Jewry, Hitler believed it was necessary for Germany to gain control over a vast empire in which Aryan supremacy could be ensured.

Hitler's Anti-Semitism

In *Mein Kampf* Hitler argued that the Jew undermined the racial purity of the German people:

> The black-haired Jewish youth lies in wait for hours on end, satanically glaring at and spying on the unsuspicious girl whom

> he plans to seduce, adulterating her blood and removing her from the bosom of her own people. The Jew uses every possible means to undermine the racial foundations of a subjugated people. In his systematic efforts to ruin women and girls, he strives to break down the final barriers of discrimination between him and other peoples. The Jews were responsible for bringing Negroes into the Rhineland, with the ultimate intention of bastardizing the white race which they hate and thus lowering its cultural and political level so that the Jew might dominate. For as long as a people remain racially pure and are conscious of the treasure of their blood, they can never be conquered by the Jew. Never in this world can the Jew become the master of any people except a bastardized people.[1]

Once the Nazis gained control of the government, they pursued their racist objectives by swiftly curtailing civil liberties. In 1933 all political parties were eliminated; strikes were forbidden; and trade unions were dissolved. The arrest of dissident scholars and scientists was followed by a purge of the party's radicals. During the next few years, Jews were eliminated from the civil service, the legal and medical professions, and cultural and educational institutions. In September 1935 the Nuremberg Laws made Jews into second-class inhabitants, and all marriage and sexual liaisons were described as crimes against the state. In 1938 Jewish communal bodies were put under the control of the Gestapo, and Jews were forced to register their property. Later in the year the Nazi Party organized an onslaught against the Jewish population in which Jews were murdered and Jewish property was destroyed. This event, Kristallnacht, was a prelude to the Holocaust.

The first stage of the Nazi's plan for European Jewry began with the invasion of Poland in September 1939. In every conquered town and village, the Germans forced Jews to clear rubble, carry heavy loads, hand over jewellery, and scrub floors and lavatories with their prayer shawls. More than 600,000 Jews were forcibly moved into central ghettos ('General Government'), which effectively comprised a huge labour camp. Here Jews worked all day, seven days a week, dressed in rags and fed on bread, soup and potatoes. This slave-labour operation was, in itself, a form of murder, thousands dying of starvation, disease or exhaustion.

The Ghetto

The largest ghetto created by the Nazis was in Warsaw. One of those who visited the Warsaw ghetto provided a chilling account of its residents:

> The majority are nightmare figures, ghosts of former human beings, miserable destitutes, pathetic remnants of former humanity. One is most affected by the characteristic change which one sees in their faces: as a result of misery, poor nourishment, the lack of vitamins, fresh air and exercise, the numerous cares, worries, anticipated misfortunes, suffering and sickness, their faces have taken on a skeletal appearance. The prominent bones around their eye sockets, the yellow facial colour, the slack pendulous skin, the alarming emaciation and sickliness. And, in addition, this miserable frightened, restless, apathetic and resigned expression, like that of a hunted animal.[2]

The next stage of the plan of extermination began with the invasion of Russia in 1941. This was designed to destroy what was described by the Nazis as the 'Jewish-Bolshevik conspiracy. At first, mobile killing battalions of 500–900 men (the *Einsatzgruppen*) began the slaughter of Russian Jewry. Throughout the country the *Einsatzgruppen* moved into Russian towns, sought out the rabbi or Jewish council and obtained a list of all Jewish inhabitants. The Jews were then rounded up in marketplaces, crowded into trains, buses and trucks, and taken to the woods, where mass graves had been dug. There they were machine-gunned to death. Other methods were also employed by the Nazis. Mobile gas vans were sent to each battalion of the *Einsatzgruppen*. Meanwhile, these mobile killing operations were being supplemented by the use of fixed centres, the death camps. Six of the most notorious of these were at Chelmno and Auschwitz in the Polish territories, and at Treblinka, Sobibor, Majdanek and Belzec in the Polish 'General Government'. In the face of such a powerful enemy the Jewish community in Europe was doomed to mass destruction. Nearly nine million Jews were resident in European countries under German control. Of those it is estimated that the Nazis killed about six million. In Poland more than 90 per cent were killed. The same percentage of the Jewish population died in the Baltic states, Germany and Austria. More than 70 per cent were murdered in the Bohemian protectorate, Slovakia, Greece, and the Netherlands, and over 50 per cent in White Russia, the Ukraine, Belgium, Yugoslavia, Romania and Norway. The six major death camps constituted the main areas of killing: over two million died at Auschwitz; 1,380,000 at Majdanek, 800,000 at Treblinka, 600,000 at Belzec; 340,000 at Chelmno; and 250,000 at Sobibor.

Arrival at the Camps

When trains arrived at the camps, terrible scenes took place. According to one of the deportees from Lvov to Belzec, the entire area of the camp was occupied by the SS:

The train entered a yard which measured about one kilometre by one kilometre and was surrounded by barbed wire and fencing about two metres high, which was not electrified. Entry to the yard was through a wooden gate covered with barbed wire. Next to the gate there was a guard house with a telephone and standing in front of the house were several SS men with dogs. When the train entered the yard the SS men closed the gate and went into the guard house. At that moment dozens of SS men opened the doors of the wagons shouting 'Out!' They pushed people out with their whips and rifles. The doors of the wagons were about one metre from the ground.

The people hurried along with blows from whips, were forced to jump down, old and young alike. It made no difference. They broke arms and legs, but they had to obey the orders of the SS men.[3]

The terrors of the Nazi regime profoundly influenced Jewish consciousness. Increasingly, world Jewry was convinced of the necessity of establishing a Jewish state as a safe haven from further atrocities, and, as outlined in the previous chapter, on 29 November 1947 the General Assembly voted in favour of the creation of a Jewish homeland in Palestine. In May of the following year the British indicated that they would continue to rule Palestine until 15 May 1948 when the British Mandate would come to an end. Despite the threat of Arab attack, on 14 May 1948 in Tel Aviv David Ben-Gurion and other leaders put their signatures to Israel's Declaration of Independence. As we have seen, the document opened by describing the Land of Israel as the birthplace of the Jewish people, and looked back to the Jewish past. It went on to explain that the Jewish people had prayed and hoped for their return to the land of their ancestors, and had striven in every generation to re-establish themselves in their ancient homeland. In recent times they had returned as pioneers and defenders and had re-created a thriving community. Recounting the stages of historical development, the Declaration emphasized the destruction of European Jewry under the Nazi regime and the urgency in light of this of creating a Jewish nation. Although the Jewish state was universally rejected by the Arab world, Israel has determinedly defended itself from its enemies, and continues to serve as a source of inspiration and hope for Jews scattered throughout the world.

Holocaust Denial

To the dismay of the Jewish community, in the years following the Second World War a range of revisionist historians have been adamant that the Holocaust never took place. In their view, the attempt to annihilate the Jewish people did not occur. Further, they insist that if any side was culpable during the Second World War, it was not the Germans; rather the real crimes against humanity were committed by the Americans, Russians, British and French. According to these Holocaust deniers, the Jewish community has perpetrated the myth of the Holocaust for its own purposes. Jews, they claim, were not victims of the Nazis – instead they stole billions of dollars in reparations, destroyed Germany's reputation, and gained worldwide support for the creation of a Jewish state.

One of the earliest proponents of Holocaust denial was Maurice Bardèche, who argued in Nuremberg that some of the evidence regarding the concentration camps was falsified. In his view, many of the deaths that took place there were the result of starvation and illness. Further, he maintained that the term 'Final Solution' referred to the transfer of Jews to ghettos in the East. A second figure who contributed to this early debate was Paul Rassinier; in *Le Passage de la Ligne* he attempted to demonstrate that survivors' claims about the Nazis were not reliable. According to Rassinier, survivors exaggerated what had occurred to them. In a later work, *The Drama of European Jewry*, he asserted that the alleged genocide of European Jewry was a myth. The gas chambers, he claimed, were an invention of the Zionists. He also stressed that the testimonies of Nazi leaders tried of war crimes should be discounted because they were testifying under the threat of death, and they therefore confessed what they thought would most likely save their lives. In Rassinier's view, those responsible for such falsification were the Zionists, aided by Jewish historians and institutions that conducted research on the Holocaust. Such fraud was motivated by the desire for financial remuneration.

Turning to Hitler, Rassinier was intent on demonstrating that, despite contradictory evidence, the Fuhrer had no intention of destroying the Jewish population of Europe. All seeming references to such annihilation, he argued, were hyperbolic declarations. There was, he believed, no explicit evidence that could prove the Nazis' intention was to murder Jewry. In this connection, he stressed that Hitler's speeches were not used as evidence at the Nuremberg Trials. It was the media, controlled by Zionists, that fostered this falsification of the Nazi past.

In the late 1950s Austin J. App maintained that far less then six million Jews died during the Nazi regime. A defender of Nazi Germany, he formulated eight axioms in *The Six Million Swindle*, which have served as the guiding principles of Holocaust denial:

1. Emigration, never annihilation, was the Reich's plan for solving Germany's Jewish problem. Had Germany intended to annihilate all the Jews, a half-million concentration camp inmates would not have survived and managed to come to Israel, where they collect 'fancy indemnities from West Germany'.

2. 'Absolutely no Jews were gassed in a concentration camps in Germany, and evidence is piling up that none were gassed in Auschwitz.' The Hitler gas chambers never existed. The gassing installations found in Auschwitz were really crematoria for cremating corpses of those who had died from a variety of causes, including the 'genocidic' Anglo-American bombing raids.

3. The majority of Jews who disappeared and remain unaccounted for did so in territories under Soviet, not German, control.

4. The majority of Jews who supposedly died while in German hands were, in fact, subversives, partisans, spies, saboteurs, and criminals or victims of unfortunate but internationally legal reprisals.

5. If there existed the slightest likelihood that the Nazis had really murdered six million Jews, world Jewry would demand subsidies to conduct research on the topic and Israel would open its archives to historians. They have not done so. Instead they have persecuted and branded as an anti-Semite anyone who wished to publicize the hoax. This persecution constitutes the most conclusive evidence that the six million figure is a 'swindle'.

6. The Jews and the media who exploit this figure have failed to offer

even a shred of evidence to prove it. The Jews misquote Eichmann and other Nazis in order to try to substantiate their claims.

7. It is the accusers, not the accused, who must provide the burden of proof to substantiate the six million figure. The Talmudists and Bolsheviks have so browbeaten the Germans that they pay billions and do not dare to demand proof.

8. The fact that Jewish scholars themselves have 'ridiculous' discrepancies in their calculations of the number of victims constitutes firm evidence that there is no scientific proof to this accusation.[4]

Holocaust denial was promoted later in the 1970s by Arthur Butz. In his *The Hoax of the Twentieth Century*, Butz argued that the Jewish people had perpetrated the hoax of the Holocaust to further Zionism. In Butz's opinion, the Holocaust myth was promoted by a conspiratorial group of Zionists who were intent on gaining sympathy and support for Israel. Banding together, Jews worldwide had used their considerable power to foster the belief that millions of Jews died at the hands of the Nazis. In pursuit of this aim, masses of documents were forged as evidence of the Nazi crime against the Jewish people. Such forgeries included reports by *Einsatzgruppen* commanders, official communiqués by high-ranking members of the Third Reich and speeches by Nazi leaders. Butz also cast doubt on the testimony of those accused of war crimes by insisting that such declarations were less reliable than documentary evidence. Further, he claimed that such testimonies were extracted through torture, or that defendants fabricated statements in the hope of saving their lives.

Over the next few decades, Holocaust denial became a central theme of historical revisionists, who sought to discredit previous studies of the Holocaust. The historian David Irving, for example, repeatedly argued that Israel swindled billions of marks in voluntary reparations from West Germany. The gas chambers, he maintained, were a myth promulgated by Jews. Tracing the origins of this myth to the British Psychological Warfare Executive, he stated that it was used in 1942 to spread false propaganda that the Germans were using gas chambers to kill Jews and others.

Holocaust Denial

Within the Jewish world, Holocaust denial has been bitterly condemned as a modern manifestation of hatred of the Jewish community. One of the main critics of historical revisionism, the historian Deborah Lipstadt, noted in *Denying the Holocaust: The Growing Assault on Truth and Memory*:

> If Holocaust denial has demonstrating anything, it is the fragility of memory, truth, reason and history. The deniers' campaign has been carefully designed to take advantage of these vulnerabilities … Right-wing nationalist groups in Germany, Austria, France, Norway, Hungary, Brazil, Slovakia and a broad array of other countries, including the United States, have adopted Holocaust denial as a standard facet of their propaganda. Whereas these groups once justified the murder of the Jews, now they deny it. Once they argued that something quite beneficial to the world happened at Auschwitz. Now they insist nothing did. Their anti-Semitism is often so virulent that the logical conclusion of their argument is that though Hitler did not murder the Jews, he should have.[5]

Religious Faith after the Holocaust

In the decades following the Holocaust, the Jewish community was preoccupied with a variety of issues: the creation of a Jewish state, rebuilding Jewish communities in Europe, and revitalizing Jewish life throughout the world. It was not until some time later that Jewish thinkers began to struggle with the religious perplexities raised by the death of millions of Jews. The Third Reich's system of murder squads, concentration camps and killing centres brought about a re-evaluation of the Jewish understanding of God's action in the world.

One of the first writers to grapple with this issue was the Jewish scholar and Conservative rabbi Richard Rubenstein. In *After Auschwitz* he argues that the most important issue for the Jewish community arises out of the question of God and the destruction of six million Jews at the hands of the Nazis. According to Rubenstein, it is no longer possible to believe in a supernatural Deity who acts in history. Rather, the Holocaust has demonstrated that such a belief has no foundation. Jews today, he contends, live in the time of the death of God.

The Death of God

In *After Auschwitz*, Richard Rubenstein argued that the Nazi death camps are a decisive refutation of the belief in a loving providential Deity:

> The agony of European Jewry cannot be likened to the testing of Job. To see any purpose in the death camps, the traditional believer is forced to regard the most demonic, anti-human explosion of all history as a meaningful expression of God's purposes. The idea is simply too obscene for me to accept … When I say we live in the time of the death of God, I mean that the thread uniting God and man, heaven and earth, has been broken. We stand in a cold, silent, unfeeling cosmos, unaided by any powerful power beyond our own resources. After Auschwitz, what else can a Jew say about God?[6]

Such disenchantment permeates the writings of the Jewish novelist Elie Wiesel. In his novel *Night*, he describes his despair in the camps. As he explains, religious doubt set in as he experienced the horrors of the Nazi regime. Describing such scenes of terror, he portrays the evolution of his religious protest. Such rebellion was heightened during the High Holy Days. Unable to pray, Wiesel became the accuser. On the Day of Atonement, he refused to fast. He no longer accepted God's silence in the face of suffering and murder.

The Renewal of Faith

Other Jews, however, reaffirmed their faith despite the camps, or, in some cases, even affirmed it *within* them. In an anthology, *Hasidic Tales of the Holocaust*, the Jewish scholar Yaffa Eliach records the testimony of those who faced death with confidence. As she explains, Hasidim expressed courage in ghettos, hiding places and camps. For these pious Jews, religious faith sustained them, providing the inner strength necessary to endure the horrors of the Nazi era. Some of these Hasidim attempted to justify God's providential plan for his chosen people. Others related the Holocaust to the suffering prior to the coming of the Messiah. Another response focused on the sanctification of God in life in defiance of the Nazi aim to exterminate the Jewish people.

In a similar vein, a number of post-Holocaust Jewish writers attempted to understand the Holocaust as part of God's providential plan for the Jewish nation. In *With Fury Poured Out*, for example, the Orthodox Jewish writer Bernard Maza contends that God brought about the Holocaust in order to revive Jewish life in a post-Enlightenment world. An alternative approach is outlined in *The Face of God after Auschwitz* by the Reform Jewish theologian Ignaz Maybaum. He argues here that the Holocaust was part of God's providential plan, serving as the means whereby medieval institutions of Jewish life were eliminated in the Nazi onslaught against European Jewry. Hitler thus served as a divine instrument for the reconstruction of Jewish existence in the twentieth century. Jewish progress, therefore, is the direct result of this modern catastrophe.

Arguing along different lines, a number of Orthodox thinkers have attempted to make sense of the Holocaust in terms of God's aim for the Jewish nation. In an essay 'Hester Panim in the Holocaust versus the Manifest Miracles in our Generation', Sha'ar Yashuv Cohen, the Chief Rabbi of Haifa, maintains that it is a mistake to believe that the Holocaust is a punishment for sin. Rather, the murder of millions of Jews in the camps should be understood as part of God's plan. The suffering of Jewry, he argues, should be seen as the last phase of the birth pangs of the Messiah. Those who were sent to the gas chambers singing 'I believe with perfect faith in the coming of the Messiah' were aware that they were living in the last days prior to divine deliverance.

For other thinkers, however, the Holocaust remains a mystery which cannot be explained. In *What Do Jews Believe?* the Jewish writer David Ariel maintains that there is simply no way that the Holocaust can be made sense of. God's will is unfathomable. In this regard, he refers to God's response to Job. Although we can empathize with Job's suffering, it is impossible to understand God's will. The mystery of how God could have permitted the murder of millions of innocent victims remains inexplicable. Nonetheless, we must acknowledge the depth of evil perpetrated by the Nazis and ensure that such atrocities are prevented in the future. Arguing along similar lines in *Sacred Fragments*, the Jewish theologian Neil Gillman writes that all theodicies proposed by Jewish scholars fail to answer the problem posed by the events of the Nazi regime.

Divine Mystery

In *What Do Jews Believe?*, David Ariel argues that there can be no rational explanation for the terrible events of the Nazi regime. In his view, God's purposes are unfathomable:

> God's answer to Job is the classical answer of Judaism to the question of human suffering. God is transcendent and his nature is unknowable. We can relate to Job's anguish and loneliness. God's silence about the fairness or injustice of his fate leaves him in a state of religious despair. Trust in God can never be again taken for granted. Yet the voice within the tempest strangely brings Job the desolate peace of a man who accepts his fate and the abyss between human and divine understanding. The very existence of God as creator of the universe gives our lives meaning. The only way to make life bearable when we cannot find answers is to recognize that some answers are beyond us.[7]

Divine Suffering and Free Will

Drawing on the theme of human suffering, other theologians have focused on the nature of divine suffering during the Holocaust. The Jewish philosopher Hans Jonas argues in 'The Concept of God after Auschwitz' that the traditional concept of divine impassibility should be set aside in the post-Holocaust period. Today, it should be acknowledged that God is not omnipotent. Rather He is limited and suffers when human beings are overwhelmed by evil. In his view, God was present in the camps and suffered along with those who endured pain and death. It is a mistake to think that He was detached from the tragedies that took place during the Nazi reign of terror.

Echoing such sentiments, the Hasidic writer Kalonymus Kalman Shapira, in *The Holy Fire*, maintains that God suffers on behalf of his chosen people. Jewish sacred literature, he states, affirms that when a Jew is afflicted, God suffers much more than the person concerned. God, he continues, is to be found in his inner chambers weeping; when one comes close to him, one weeps as well. Through this encounter an individual is strengthened so that he or she can study and worship. This understanding serves as a framework for coming to terms with the horrors of the Nazi regime.

Linked to this conception of divine suffering is the view that the religious perplexities posed by the Holocaust can be solved by appealing to the free-will argument. In *Faith after the Holocaust*, the Orthodox theologian Eliezer Berkovits asserts that if God did not respect human freedom, then men and women would cease to be human. Freedom and responsibility are the preconditions of human life. Hence, the Holocaust should be understood as a manifestation of evil, a tragedy inflicted by the Germans on the Jewish people. God did not intervene because He had bestowed free will on human beings at the time of creation.

Divine Providence and Free Will

In *Faith after the Holocaust* Eliezer Berkovits argues that religious belief is possible after the nightmare of the crematoria. In his view the problem of faith can be solved by appealing to the free-will argument:

> The hiding God is present; though man is unaware of him, He is present in his hiddenness. Therefore, God can only hide in this world. But if this world were altogether and radically profane, there would be no place in it for Him to hide. He can only hide in history. Since history is man's responsibility, one would, in fact, expect him to hide, to be silent, while man is about his God-given task. Responsibility requires freedom, but God's convincing presence would undermine the freedom of human decision. God hides in human responsibility and human freedom.[8]

For Jonathan Sacks, the Chief Rabbi of Great Britain, the questions raised by the tragedy of the Holocaust must be faced by contemporary writers. Drawing on the writings of Eliezer Berkovits, he similarly argues, in *Tradition in an Untraditional Age*, that the Holocaust was the result of free choice. In his opinion, the murder of six million innocent victims illustrates that human beings are capable of the most horrendous acts. It is a mistake to blame God for this tragedy. Because human beings have been given the freedom to choose to be good, they are free also to choose evil. God does not intervene to curtail such freedom. Even though all powerful, He exercises self-restraint so as not to undermine the freedom He bestowed at creation.

In 'The Exile of the Word: From the Silence of the Bible to the Silence of Auschwitz', the Jewish scholar André Neher maintains that after Auschwitz there can only be silence. The Holocaust cannot be explained. Nonetheless, the death camps illustrate the importance of human freedom. By creating human beings free, God introduced into the universe a degree of uncertainty – both angelic and bestial actions became a possibility. In this light, it is a mistake to blame God for the existence of human suffering.

Echoing this view, the Jewish scholar David Birnbaum insists in *God and Evil* that Jews must transcend their dependence on God. They must acknowledge that God allows the exercise of personal freedom. According to Birnbaum, God has granted human beings the freedom to achieve ascending levels of spiritual maturity. The Nazis, however, chose the path of radical evil.

The Holocaust and Human Evil

In the writings of a number of Jewish theologians, an alternative theme has been stressed, which focuses on human evil. Responding to the question 'where was God at Auschwitz?', the former Chief Rabbi of Great Britain, Immanuel Jakobovits, states in 'Where was Man at Auschwitz?' that the most important issue of the Holocaust is: where was man? Where was human morality amidst the horrors of the Nazi regime? The question remains a live one, for even though Auschwitz was finally liberated from Nazi barbarians, neo-fascists are still prevalent in Western and Eastern Europe. Fifty years on, the legacy of Auschwitz continues.

In the view of the Reform rabbi Jack Bemporad, human beings are neither inherently good nor evil. In 'The Concept of Man after Auschwitz', he argues that men and women are capable of acting ethically or of behaving in the most immoral manner. The Holocaust has demonstrated that human beings are capable of the mass-murder of others. Nonetheless, it has not shown that human beings are by nature evil. Instead, it illustrates the potential each person has to sin. According to Bemporad, we must seek to preserve the human potentiality for good and foster those personal and social elements that make for personal integration.

In 'The Meaning of this Hour', the Jewish theologian Abraham Joshua Heschel points out that the world was plunged into darkness during the Nazi regime. What is now required is for men and women to assume responsibility for their actions. God, he contends, will return to us when we let him in through righteous endeavours. Such a vision animated the prophets and rabbis, who dreamed of a society free from ignorance and sin, and it must serve as a hope for the future.

The Jewish scholar Nicholas de Lange argues in *Jesus Christ and Auschwitz* that Jews and Christians need to acknowledge the different ways in which their sinfulness was responsible for the Nazi period. In confronting the question 'where was Jesus at Auschwitz?', we must recognize the complexity of this question and listen attentively to Jesus who says: 'forgive our sins'. Our failure, as much as that of others, helped to make the tragedy of the Holocaust possible.

According to the Jewish theologian Marc Ellis in *Toward a Jewish Theology of Liberation*, Israel is guilty of committing crimes against humanity. Now that the Jewish people are empowered in their own country, they are capable of suppressing the rights of the Palestinian population in their midst just as Jews were oppressed by the Nazis. Jews in Israel and the diaspora must acknowledge this paradoxical reversal of events and strive to liberate the Palestinian people from their suffering.

The Holocaust and Jewish Survival

For many Jews who faced the rise of Nazism, the quest for Jewish survival was of central importance. In his 1933 article 'Wear the Yellow Badge with Pride', the German Zionist Robert Weltsch perceived the onslaught against German Jewry as a challenge for German Jews to reassess their future. In his opinion, the only solution to the problem of anti-Semitism was for Jews to settle in Palestine. God would not intervene to save his people from the Nazis. Instead, they would have to save themselves.

In contemporary society, a number of Jewish theologians have stressed the theme of Jewish survival in their reflections on the Holocaust. The Jewish philosopher Emil Fackenheim, for example, in his essay 'Jewish Faith and the Holocaust' argues that God issued the 614th commandment out of the ashes of Auschwitz: thou shalt not grant Hitler a posthumous victory. Jews are commanded to survive as Jews lest the Jewish people perish. They are obliged as well to remember the victims of Auschwitz lest their memory perish. In addition, they are forbidden to despair of humanity and the world, lest they cooperate in delivering the world over to the forces of Auschwitz.

The Commanding Voice

In 'Jewish Faith and the Holocaust', Emil Fackenheim argues that God was present in the death camps. Out of the ashes of Auschwitz, He issued the 614th commandment:

> Jews are forbidden to hand Hitler posthumous victories. They are commanded to survive as Jews lest the Jewish people perish. They are commanded to remember the victims of Auschwitz lest

their memory perish. They are forbidden to despair of man and his world, and to escape into either cynicism or otherworldliness, lest they cooperate in delivering the world over to the forces of Auschwitz. Finally, they are forbidden to despair of the God of Israel, lest Judaism perish.[9]

Drawing on the writings of Emil Fackenheim, the Jewish writer Lionel Rubinoff outlines in his essay 'Auschwitz and the Theology of the Holocaust' what he believes to be an authentic response to the Nazi era. In his view, Jews must remain loyal to their tradition, and thereby ensure that Judaism continues in the future. How, he asks, can a Jew respond Jewishly to an event like Auschwitz? Jews can only respond by dedicating themselves to survival in the age of the death camps. Jews today, he insists, must confront the demons of Auschwitz and prevail against them. Given that there is no solution to the theological problems raised by the Holocaust, one must simply remain faithful to the tradition.

In *Toward a Jewish Theology*, the Jewish scholar Byron Sherwin contends that American and Israeli Jews have focused on acts of resistance under Nazi rule rather than martyrdom. Yet this shift in emphasis is what led to the abandonment of spiritual ideals. According to Sherwin, the primary values of Judaism are embodied in its religious message, ethical lifestyle and theological beliefs. Jewish survival is not an end in itself.

Echoing this view, the Jewish scholar Michael Goldberg explores the ways in which the Holocaust has influenced contemporary Jewish life. In *Why Should Jews Survive?* he observes that Jews in contemporary society fervently proclaim the message of Jewish survival. Yet, in doing so, they have overlooked the reason for such survival: the belief that God will redeem humanity. The kaddish (Jewish prayer for the dead), he states, gives voice to why Jews should survive: they constitute the hope of the world.

Fiercely rejecting the claims of Holocaust deniers, the Jewish community has determinedly commemorated the Holocaust through the establishment of Holocaust Memorial Day (Yom Ha-Shoah). Yom Ha-Shoah was inaugurated in 1951 in a law signed by the Prime Minister of Israel David Ben-Gurion and the President of Israel Yitzhak Ben-Zvi. The original proposal was to hold Yom Ha-Shoah on the 14th of Nisan, the anniversary of the Warsaw ghetto uprising on 19 April 1943. However, this was rejected because the 14th of Nisan is the day immediately before Passover. As a result, the day was moved to the 27th of Nisan, eight days before Israel Independence Day. While there are a number of Orthodox Jews who commemorate the Holocaust on Yom Ha-Shoah, others in the Orthodox world, including the Haredim, remember the victims of the Holocaust on days of mourning declared by rabbis before the Holocaust such as Tisha B'Av.

Most Jewish communities hold a solemn ceremony on this day, but there is no formal ritual. Lighting memorial candles and reciting the kaddish are common. In Israel the Conservative movement has created Megillat Ha-Shoah, a scroll and liturgical reading. On the eve of Yom Ha-Shoah, in Israel, there is a state ceremony at Yad Vashem, the Holocaust Martyrs' and Heroes' Remembrance Authority. Air-raid sirens are sounded for two minutes. During this time people stop what they are doing and stand at attention. On the eve of Yom Ha-Shoah and the day itself, places of public entertainment are closed, and Israeli television screens Holocaust documentaries and talk-shows. Flags on public buildings are flown at half-mast. In the diaspora, Jews who observe Yom Ha-Shoah do so within the synagogue as well as in the Jewish community. Commemorations range from religious services to communal vigils and educational programmes, often featuring a talk by a Holocaust survivor. In some communities the names of Holocaust victims are recited, emphasizing the human cost of this tragedy.

The State of Israel and Arab–Israeli Conflict

The Holocaust and the establishment of the State of Israel were organically related events – the death of millions of Jews in the Second World War profoundly affected Jewry throughout the world. Some traditional Jews believed that the Holocaust was a punishment upon the community because of its sins but would be followed by the founding of a Jewish state. Others thought the creation of Israel was the consequence of Jewish suffering.

Whatever the cause, Hitler's policy unintentionally assisted the Jewish community in Palestine: 60,000 Jews left Germany for Israel and contributed substantially to the growth and development of a homeland. In addition, as we noted in Chapter 2, from the beginning of the war in 1939, the creation of a Jewish state became the primary aim of Zionists. In order to achieve this objective the Jewish community had to persuade the Allies of the virtues of their plan. As far as the British were concerned, though the Balfour Declaration of 1917 supported the establishment of a Jewish homeland in Palestine, the 1939 MacDonald White Paper effectively rejected this proposal and projected a future in which there would be no predominately Jewish presence.

The Peel Commission

The Peel Commission of 1937 had proposed a partition of Palestine into a Jewish and an Arab state. The Jewish portion was to include the following:

Starting from Ras al-Naqura it follows the existing northern and eastern frontier of Palestine to Lake Tiberias and crosses the lake to the outflow of the River Jordan whence it continues down the river to a point a little north of Beisan. It then cuts across the Beisan Plain and runs along to the southern edge of the valley of Jezreel and across the plain of Jezreel to a point near Megiddo, whence it crosses the Carmel ridge in the neighbourhood of the Megiddo road. Having thus reached the Maritime Plain the line runs southward down its eastern edge until it reaches the Jerusalem–Joppa corridor near Lydda. South of the corridor it continues down the edge of the plain to a point about ten miles south of Rehovot whence it turns west to the sea.[10]

During the war and afterwards, the British steadfastly maintained this policy and prevented illegal immigrants from entering the Holy Land. In the Jews' struggle against the British, Menachem Begin, the leader of the Revisionists' military arm (the Irgun) played an important role. Similarly, an extremist group called the Stern Gang, which broke away from the Irgun, carried on a campaign against British domination. Eventually, the British resolved to leave Palestine, and the United Nations sought to resolve the conflict through a policy of partition in which there would be a Jewish and an Arab state as well as an international zone in Jerusalem. Once the UN plan for partition was endorsed, the Arabs began to attack Jewish settlements. By March 1948 over 1,000 Jews had been killed, but in the next month David Ben-Gurion ordered the Haganah to link up all the Jewish enclaves and consolidate the territory given to Israel under the UN partition plan. Once a government of Israel was formed, Egyptian air raids began. A truce lasting a month was formalized on 11 June 1948 during which time the Arabs reinforced their armies. When the fighting began again on 9 July, the Israelis appeared to be in control – they took Lydda, Ramleh and Nazareth as well as large territories beyond the partition borders.

A Jewish State in Palestine

Under David Ben-Gurion the Jews in Palestine consolidated their position, and on 14 May 1948 the independence of the Jewish state in Palestine was declared:

> Inside the auditorium, behind the dais, hung a huge photograph of Theodor Herzl. The Philharmonic Orchestra played Hatikva which had been made the new state's national anthem. Then I held in my hand the Declaration, which I read with a heart filled at once with trepidation and exultation. I tried to overcome my emotion and read the Declaration in a loud clear tone, as everybody rose to hear it. Rabbi Maimon, the doyen of us all, recited the blessing thanking the Almighty for 'sustaining us so that we have lived to see this day ...' Everybody present signed. I announced the State of Israel was now in existence and the meeting was adjourned. In the streets the throngs sang and danced.[11]

Though the Arabs agreed to a truce, there were outbursts of violence, and in October 1948 the Israelis launched an offensive that resulted in the capture of Beersheba. On 12 January 1949 armistice talks were held and later signed with Egypt, Lebanon, Transjordan and Syria. During this period more than 650,000 Arab inhabitants of Palestine escaped from Israeli-held territory: 280,000 to the West Bank; 70,000 to Transjordan; 100,000 to Lebanon; 4,000 to Iraq; 75,000 to Syria; 7,000 to Egypt; and 190,000 to the Gaza Strip.

Mindful of these Palestinian refugees, the Arabs regarded the armistice as merely a temporary truce. Under President Nasser of Egypt, a plan for the elimination of the Jewish state was put into operation. From 1956, President Gamal Abdel Nasser refused Israeli ships access to the Gulf of Aqaba; in April he signed a pact with Saudi Arabia and Yemen; in July he seized the Suez Canal; in October he formed a military command with Jordan and Syria. In response Israel launched a strike on 19 October, conquering Sinai and opening the sea route to Aqaba. In an agreement that ended the fighting, Israel undertook to withdraw from Sinai provided that Egypt did not remilitarize it and UN forces constituted a cordon sanitaire. This arrangement existed for a decade, though armed struggle between both sides continued.

In 1967 Nasser began another offensive against Israel. On 15 May he moved 100,000 troops into the Sinai and ordered the UN forces to leave. He then blockaded Aqaba by closing the Tiran Straits to Israeli shipping and signed a military agreement with King Hussein of Jordan. On 5 June the Israelis launched a pre-emptive strike devastating the Egyptian air force on the ground. Jordan and Syria then entered the war on Egypt's side. Two days later Israel captured the West Bank. During the next two days Israel attacked the Golan Heights and reoccupied Sinai.

The Six Day War was a major victory for the Israelis but did not bring security to the Jewish state. In July 1972, President Anwar Sadat of Egypt expelled Egypt's Soviet advisers, cancelled the political and military alliances that Nasser had made with other Arab states and, together with Syria, attacked Israel. Then, on Yom Kippur, 6 October 1973, he attacked Israel. The Egyptian and Syrian forces broke through Israeli lines and serious losses were inflicted on Israeli planes and armour. On 9 October the Syrian advance was halted, and the next day the American President Richard Nixon began an airlift of weapons. Two days later the Israelis mounted a counterattack against Egypt – this was a turning point in the conflict and a ceasefire came into force on 14 October 1973.

During this period and for the next few years, the Israeli government was led by a Labour-dominated coalition, but in May 1977 the Likud Party led by Menachem Begin came to power. On 9 November 1977 President Sadat offered to negotiate peace terms with Israel, which were formalized at Camp David on 5 September 1978. Under the terms of this agreement, Egypt recognized Israel's right to exist, and provided guarantees for Israel's southern border; in return, Israel gave back Sinai, undertook to negotiate away much of the West Bank, and made concessions over Jerusalem in exchange for a complementary treaty with the Palestinians and other Arab peoples. These later terms, however, were not realized since the plan was rejected by the Palestinian Arabs.

The capital of Israel

In 1967, in the Six Day War, Jerusalem was captured by the Israeli forces. Despite international pressure, in 1980 it was proclaimed the capital of Israel:

1. Jerusalem whole and united is the capital of Israel.
2. Jerusalem is the seat of the President of the State, the Knesset, the Government and the Supreme Court.

3. The Holy places shall be protected from desecration and any other offence and from anything likely to prejudice the freedom of access of the members of the different religions to the places sacred to them or their feelings with regard to those places.[12]

In the 1980s Israel attempted to combat the menace of the Palestine Liberation Organization, which continually threatened Israeli security. From 6 June 1982 the Israel Defence Forces (IDF) launched an offensive against the PLO in southern Lebanon; this occupation involved heavy bombing, which resulted in massive Arab casualties. In addition, Muslim refugees were slaughtered by Christian Falangist Arabs in the Sabra and Shatilla refugee camps on 16 September 1982. Both the invasion of Lebanon and this massacre provoked discord between Israel and her allies as well as controversy in Israel.

By 1987 the Palestinians in the Occupied Territories were largely young educated people who had benefited from formal education. Yet, despite such educational advances, they suffered from limited job expectations and this situation led to political radicalism. As hostilities increased, the intifada (resistance) demonstrated that occupying the West Bank and the Gaza Strip would be a perpetual problem. From the Israeli side, the Israeli Defence Forces viewed the intifada in the context of Israel's relationship with its Palestinian neighbours and the world in general. In April 1989 the Israeli police reported that they had uncovered a network of illegal classes held by two West Bank universities at private schools in East Jerusalem. As the intifada intensified, Yitzhak Rabin recommended that elections should take place in the West Bank and the Gaza Strip. This peace initiative, however, was dependent on several conditions: Israel would negotiate only with Palestinians not connected with the PLO and who resided in the occupied territories, and there would be no change in the status of the occupied territories. Such conditions were not acceptable to the PLO, and as a consequence the intifada continued.

On 1 August 1990 the Iraqi leader Saddam Hussein decided to invade Kuwait. Joining with the United States, Israel demanded Iraq's withdrawal. On 17 January 1991 a coalition of Allied forces attacked the Iraqi army. Israel, however, was not encouraged to participate in this conflict. Eventually, Saddam was defeated, and the intifada continued. Throughout the next year, diplomatic negotiations took place to find a solution to the Palestinian problem. Despite these steps, tension mounted in the West Bank and Jerusalem, the efforts to renew the peace process inflaming members of Hamas and Islamic Jihad, who were bitterly opposed to compromise.

Despite acts of violence on both sides, talks between Israel and the PLO began at a villa outside Oslo on 20 January 1993 and continued over the next few months. The Oslo Accords served as the framework for the peace process and a basis for Israeli–Arab cooperation. On 3 May 1994 Rabin and Arafat met in Cairo to finalize a peace agreement. This was followed by a series of meetings the next year, and throughout this period the Israeli government transferred a number of areas of government to the Palestinians in both the West Bank and the Gaza Strip. However, the peace process was disrupted with the assassination of Rabin at a rally in Jerusalem on 28 October 1995.

In the face of renewed attacks on Israel, the Oslo agreement came under increasing pressure. In the midst of uncertainty about governmental policy, an election was called. On the night before this took place, Operation Grapes of Wrath against Israel's enemies was launched. For over two weeks Israeli forces bombed fundamentalist positions north of the security zone with Lebanon. On 16 May 1996 elections took place and Benjamin Netanyahu narrowly won the election for Prime Minister.

In October 1998 Netanyahu and Yasser Arafat met in Washington to discuss the peace process. After prolonged argument, Israel and the Palestinians agreed to embark on a new stage of cooperation. According to the Wye River Memorandum, Israel would effect a further West Bank redeployment, involving 27.2 per cent of the occupied territory. Arafat agreed that the Palestinian authorities would take all measures necessary to prevent acts of terrorism, crime and hostilities. Further, they resolved to apprehend, investigate and prosecute specific individuals suspected of violence.

Determined to continue the peace process, the United States sought to persuade Palestinians and Israelis that a negotiated settlement was vital to security in the Middle East. In April 1001 the Mitchell Report was published, which made a series of wide-ranging recommendations. Nonetheless, violence continued into 2001 and 2002, despite attempts by the Mitchell Commission and others to restore peace. Then, on 11 September 2001, al-Qaeda terrorists hijacked airliners and flew them into the World Trade Center in New York and the Pentagon outside Washington. In response, President Bush warned that governments would now have to choose to support the United States in a war on terror, or be regarded as enemies.

Continuing Conflict

Following the attack on the Twin Towers of the World Trade Center and the offensive against Osama Bin Laden, Arab and Islamic countries sought to obtain concessions from Israel in return for cooperation in the war against terror. However, many Americans began to lose sympathy for the Palestinian cause, identifying Hamas and Hezbollah with the al-Qaeda group of terrorists. On 12 March 2002 the UN Security Council passed Resolution 1397, a US-drafted resolution, referring for the first time to a Palestinian state existing side by side with Israel.

Although Yasser Arafat declared a cessation of violence on numerous occasions, this did not seem to affect the frequency of suicide bombings and ambushes perpetrated against Israel. A bombing at the Park Hotel in Netanya, for example, killed 27 people. For their part, the Israelis continued with the policy of assassinating Palestinians, and, in retaliation against the Park Hotel bombing, they launched a massive raid intended to root out the Palestinian terror network, reoccupying Ramallah, Nablus, Jenin, Tulkarm and other towns. In this onslaught, referred to as Operation Defensive Shield, a significant number of Palestinians were killed. Israel's goal was to dismantle the terrorist infrastructure developed by the Palestinian Authority (PA) or allowed to operate in territory under PA control. The operation consisted of moving Israeli forces into the West Bank and Gaza for the purpose of arresting terrorists, finding and confiscating weapons, and destroying facilities for the manufacture of explosives.

Operation Defensive Shield

Defending the policy of the Israeli government, Ariel Sharon blamed Yasser Arafat for actions that had been taken against Israel:

There is one dispatcher: Palestinian Authority Chairman Yasser Arafat. He is the man who, in a series of agreements, promised to abandon the path of terrorism, refrain from committing murder, use his forces to prevent it – and betrayed all his promises. Because of his promises Israel agreed to the establishment of the Palestinian Authority. That is why Israel agreed to transfer security responsibility to the areas given to its control. Thus, Israel agreed to the establishment of Palestinian security forces. We hoped that the Palestinians would understand, as they promised, that ruling does not mean licence to kill, but

> rather the assumption of responsibility for the prevention of killing. But what was merely apprehension at the beginning, and intensified into suspicion, has turned into solid facts which nobody can deny. In the territories under his rule, Arafat has established a regime of terror, which nationally and officially trains terrorists and incites, finances, arms and sends them to perpetuate murderous operations across Israel.[13]

Despite the arrival of US Secretary of State, Colin Powell, the violence continued. Powell's mission failed; he was unable to persuade the Palestinians to agree to a ceasefire. By the time Powell left, Israel had withdrawn from some towns, but Yasser Arafat was still imprisoned in Ramallah, and the Israelis were besieging the Church of the Nativity in Bethlehem, where armed Palestinians had sought refuge. On 19 April the Security Council adopted Resolution 1405, calling for an impartial investigative team to be sent to assess the claim that Israelis had committed a massacre in the Jenin refugee camp.

On 19 April the Security Council adopted Resolution 1405 and called for an impartial investigative team to be sent to determine the truth of these claims. Although Israel at first agreed to this investigation, it later blocked it, claiming that the composition and procedures would not be impartial. In May 2002 Prime Minister Sharon visited the US under pressure from Washington; during this meeting discussions took place concerning a regional summit to be held later in 2002. By the end of May, Yasser Arafat signed into law the Basic Law or constitution of the Palestinian transitional state. This law guaranteed basic rights, but stated that Palestinian legislation would be based on the principles of Islamic Shari'a law.

The Palestinian Constitution

Beginning with a declaration that Palestine is part of the larger Arab World, and that the Palestinian people are part of the Arab nation, the Palestinian Constitution includes a series of principles governing public rights and freedoms:

Article 9. All Palestinians are equal under the law.
Article 11. It is unlawful to arrest, search, imprison, restrict the freedom or prevent the movement of any person.

Article 13. No person shall be subject to any duress or torture.

Article 14. The accused is innocent until proven guilty in a court of law.

Article 15. Punishment shall only be imposed on individuals.

Article 17. Homes shall be inviolable.

Article 18. Freedom of belief and the performance of religious rituals are guaranteed.

Article 19. Every person shall have the right to freedom of thought.

Article 21. The economic system in Palestine shall be based on the principle of free market economy.

Article 23. Proper housing is a right for every citizen.

Article 24. Every citizen has the right to education.

Article 26. Palestinians shall have the right to participate in the political life individually and in groups.

Article 28. No Palestinian may be deported from the homeland.

Article 30. Litigation is a protected and guaranteed right to all people.

Article 31. An independent commission for human rights shall be established by law.[14]

In June, following a wave of Palestinian suicide attacks, Israeli forces reoccupied the West Bank and began the construction of a security wall. Even though the Israeli government claimed that this reoccupation would not continue indefinitely, it later altered its plans. In August and September 2002, attempts were made to bring about Palestinian ceasefire initiatives, but these were opposed by extremist groups. As time passed, the Labour Party withdrew from the Israel unity government; elections were held in January and Ariel Sharon (leader of the Likud Party) was re-elected Prime Minister. In March 2003 the United States and Britain attacked Iraq, overthrowing the regime of Saddam Hussein. Prior to this conflict, President Bush reiterated his desire for a solution to the Palestinian problem in the Middle East, yet in the Arab world the onslaught against Iraq was widely perceived as a Crusade against Islam.

In the first part of the year 2003 the United States had expressed its refusal to negotiate with Yasser Arafat, and, bowing to international pressure, Arafat appointed Mahmoud Abbas (a founder member of the militant group Fatah) as the new Palestinian Prime Minister. Abbas' term as leader was characterized by various conflicts with Arafat regarding the distribution of power and with Palestinian militant groups, including Islamic Jihad and Hamas, over his moderate policies. In October 2003 Abbas resigned, citing a lack of support from Israel and the United States as well as internal incitements against his government. Responding to terrorist attacks, Israel launched Operation Rainbow in the Gaza Strip in May 2004; several months later, Operation Days of Penitence was launched in September and October 2004. In November 2004 Yasser Arafat died, and Mahmoud Abbas was elected President of the Palestinian National Authority in January 2005.

During this period, Israel's unilateral disengagement plan was adopted: the aim was to remove the permanent Israeli presence in the Gaza Strip as well as four settlements in the northern West Bank. By 12 September 2005 Israel had completed its disengagement and fully withdrawn from the Gaza Strip. In January 2006 Palestinian elections took place. Due to widespread dissatisfaction with Fatah, Hamas won a majority of seats and was thereby able to appoint a Prime Minister as well as a number of cabinet posts. Alarmed by these developments, the West branded Hamas a terrorist organization and cut off aid to the Palestinian government in March 2006, insisting that it recognize Israel, renounce violence and accept the peace process.

On 14 April 2006 Ehud Olmert was elected Prime Minister of Israel, having already been exercising the powers of the office since they were transferred to him after Ariel Sharon had suffered a stroke in December 2005 followed by a much more serious one the following month. In June 2006 a war commenced between Israel and Hezbollah when Hezbollah fighters entered Israel and attacked an IDF post, capturing several soldiers. In response Israel attacked Hezbollah positions within Lebanon. The result was that both sides agreed to a ceasefire and Lebanon stationed its army along the border with Israel.

During this period of instability, international sanctions against Hamas and the PA resulted in economic and political difficulties for the Palestinian people. On 8 October 2006 Mahmoud Abbas warned Hamas that he would call new legislative elections if it did not accept a coalition government. The following month saw efforts by Mahmoud Abbas to form a unity government with Hamas, but this produced no tangible results. On 27 November 2006 Ehud Olmert appealed to the Palestinians to re-enter peace negotiations with the aim of establishing an independent and viable Palestinian state with full sovereignty and defined borders. In December 2006 violence between Fatah and Hamas increased, leading to a virtual civil war.

In January 2007, fighting continued between Hamas and Fatah, and although a truce was negotiated at the end of the month, new fighting broke out after a few days. In February 2007 President Abbas and Prime Minister Haniyet met in Saudi Arabia to discuss the conflict. It was agreed that Hamas would dissolve the existing government and form a unity coalition with Fatah. By April 2007 Ehud Olmert had ruled out a major Gaza offensive, but he authorized the army to carry out limited operations in the Gaza Strip. This led to a new round of Hamas rocket attacks. In response Israel launched air strikes against various targets. In June 2007 full-scale fighting broke out between factions in several communities, and Hamas won control of the entire Gaza Strip, establishing a separate Gaza Strip government. Israel, the US and other Western countries replied by seeking to strengthen Fatah and thereby isolate Hamas. Although Fatah had been defeated in Gaza, it retained control of the West Bank.

In the ensuing months, steps were taken to resume the peace process. November 2007 saw Israeli and Palestinian leaders agree to restart peace talks at a Maryland summit, promising further negotiations towards a peace treaty and the development of a Palestinian state. In the same month President Bush pledged his support for Israeli–Palestinian peace efforts. By early December 2007 the first Israeli–Palestinian peace talks in seven years got off to a shaky start. At the same time, international donors pledged to support the embattled Palestinian government of President Abbas, offering billions in aid over three years. By the end of the month, a second round of negotiations took place between Palestinian and Israeli officials. Yet this event was overshadowed by Palestinian threats not to address substantive issues unless Israel agreed to stop settlement construction around Jerusalem.

Conflict between Israel and Hamas continued throughout this period, culminating in a ferocious onslaught against Gaza in an attempt to curb Hamas rocket attacks on Israel and destroy the Hamas terror infrastructure once and for all. In January 2009, following heavy air, sea and artillery bombardment, Israeli tanks and troops launched a ground invasion to reoccupy parts of the northern Gaza Strip. As Israelis tanks and infantry crossed into the area, reports emerged of fighting between Hamas and Israeli troops. .

Reaction to the Assault

Across the world, including in Israel itself, there has been bitter criticism of the Israeli offensive:

An Israeli military college has printed damning soldiers' accounts of the killing and vandalism during recent operations in Gaza. One account tells of a sniper killing a mother and children at close range whom troops had told to leave their home. Another speaker at the seminar described what he saw as the 'cold blooded murder' of a Palestinian woman. The army has defended its conduct during the Gaza offensive but said it would investigate the testimonies, which were published by the military academy at Oranim College. Graduates of the academy, who had served in Gaza, were speaking to new recruits at a seminar.[15]

Following the election of Barack Obama as President of the United States in November 2009, the situation in the Middle East looked more hopeful. Yet despite recent efforts by President Obama to resolve the conflict between Arabs and Israelis, the Middle East conflict remains as intractable as ever.

Chapter 4

Modern Jewish Movements

Through the centuries the Jewish community has been united by a common religious tradition, as highlighted in Chapter 1. However, as we observed in Chapter 2, from the time of the Enlightenment the basic beliefs and principles of the Jewish faith have been challenged. Over the last hundred years the monolithic system has undergone significant disintegration and fragmentation. As a consequence, Jewry today is divided into a variety of subgroups with their own religious identities. On the far right, Strictly Orthodox Jews adhere to the traditional way of life as outlined in Jewish legal sources. Determined to preserve their identity, these individuals isolate themselves from the main currents of modern life. Like these Strictly Orthodox Jews, modern Orthodox Jews follow Jewish law, yet they seek to combine their loyalty to the tradition with an acceptance of contemporary society. Such neo-Orthodoxy strives to achieve a positive accommodation with the modern world. Moving across the religious spectrum, Conservative, Reconstructionist, Reform and Humanistic Jews as well as a range of other Jewish groups have in their different ways attempted to reform the tradition in the light of current knowledge.

I. Strictly Orthodox Judaism

Strictly Orthodox Judaism is the branch of Judaism that adheres most strictly to Jewish law. By the eighteenth century, rabbinic authority had diminished, leading to the disintegration of the traditional Jewish heritage. Such erosion of the traditional Jewish way of life, coupled with the aims of Jewish champions of the Enlightenment, stimulated the creation of new interpretations of the faith. Orthodoxy emerged as a response to these alterations in Jewish existence.

Today, Strictly Orthodox Jews subscribe to the fundamental principles of the Jewish faith, convinced that in doing so they are fulfilling God's will. Such a commitment serves as a framework for the Orthodox way of life. For these individuals there can be no compromise with secularism. Suspicious of modernism, they are anxious to preserve the faith through a process of intensive education, beginning at an early age. For boys this is rigorous, following the traditional Jewish curriculum established centuries ago. Expectations for girls are more limited: Jewish young women are expected to become revered mothers and homemakers.

The dominant trend in Orthodoxy since the Second World War has been its increased stress on traditional Jewish values. What is required is religious zeal, observance of the commandments, and a rejection of modern culture. Throughout the Jewish world, Orthodox Jews have actively sponsored Jewish schools, synagogues, political organizations, summer camps, and a religious press. Today, most of the Strictly Orthodox reside in Israel or the United States. In Israel, religiously observant Jews make up about 15–20 per cent of the population. Increasingly, these Strictly Orthodox Jews play an important role in communal and political life. In the United States, Strictly Orthodox Jewry has been supportive of its own institutions.

The Strictly Orthodox Way of Life

Today, the Strictly Orthodox continue to subscribe to the central religious tenets of the past, believing that in doing so they are fulfilling God's will. The following gives a picture of the Sabbath celebration in a typical Strictly Orthodox home:

On Friday evening, the house was abuzz with activity. Hairdryers hummed; children shouted and stamped; there was the constant sound of running feet. An urgent message was conveyed down the intercom. A telephone call must be returned immediately because the telephone, according to Jewish law, could not be used on the Sabbath. The men returned from synagogue:

'Good Shabbos, good Shabbos!' they said. Besides the husbands there were various nephews and rabbinic students. They were all dressed in dark suits and big hats. An elegant young Hasid with a long red beard wore a magnificent strimel (fur hat) above his kaftan. The head of the house took his seat at one end of the long table and the rabbi sat at the other.

Blessings over the wine were said by every man present, one after the other. The Sabbath songs were led by the younger son-in-law. The women did not sing – they listened. And then the food was served.[1]

2. Modern Orthodox Judaism

Alongside Strictly Orthodox Judaism, a new Orthodox group emerged in the nineteenth century under the leadership of Samson Raphael Hirsch. In Hirsch's view, it is possible to remain an Orthodox Jew while being fully conversant with modern culture. This view came to be known as modern Orthodoxy or Neo-Orthodoxy. While strictly observant and accepting the doctrine of Torah MiSinai, adherents have no hesitation in dressing in current Western fashion, attending secular universities or entering the mainstream professions.

The majority of Orthodox synagogues in the United States and throughout the diaspora are of this character. In some, men and women even sit together. Although modern Orthodox Jews frequently send their children to Jewish schools, girls and boys are educated in the same classroom and follow the same curriculum. Most Modern Orthodox girls would expect to have their own professional careers, and family planning is generally accepted.

Orthodox Outreach

Following in the footsteps of Samson Raphael Hirsch, modern Orthodox rabbis seek to sustain an Orthodox lifestyle while integrating into the mainstream of contemporary society. Strictly Orthodox critics of this approach argue that such a compromise endangers the tradition. In response to such criticism, a modern Orthodox rabbi commented:

I discovered a long time ago that there are many Jews who are not prepared to be connected to the Jewish community through religion. So I became active in the wider community in the hope that if I could build a relationship with people on some other basis, they could feel more connected to what I really represented to them which is Orthodox Judaism. It was that that led me to create entities in the community with which people could identify as Jews … People say that if only I could have taken my talents and focused them on Ultra-Orthodox institutions, I could have built something that would last … What I say is: I feel a compulsion to minister to the wider community because they're here now and they need my gifts. Even terminal cancer patients need help.[2]

3. Hasidism

The most immediately recognizable group among the Orthodox are the Hasidim. The men are bearded and wear side-curls, which are twisted and tucked behind their ears, and they are invariably dressed in black – large black hat worn over a small black skull-cap, black jacket, black trousers, black shoes and socks. Their shirts are white, buttoned up to the neck and worn without a tie. Issuing forth from the waistband of their trousers are ritual fringes, which are attached to their undergarments. Female dress is less distinctive. In common with Strictly Orthodox women, women follow the rules of modesty. Their skirts cover their knees; their sleeves extend over their elbows, and their necklines are cut high. Once a woman is married she must hide her hair: it is thus customary for women to wear wigs.

Hasidism emerged during the second half of the eighteenth century under the leadership of Israel ben Eliezer, known as the Baal Shem Tov. They initiated a profound change in Jewish religious pietism. In opposition to ascetic practices, which were common among Jewish mystics, the Baal Shem Tov and his followers emphasized the omnipresence of God. Divine light, they believed, is everywhere. As the Baal Shem Tov explained: in every one of a person's troubles, physical and spiritual, even in that trouble God himself is there.

For some Hasidim, cleaving to God (devekut) in prayer is understood as the annihilation of selfhood and the ascent of the soul to divine light. In this context, joy, humility, gratitude and spontaneity are seen as essential features of Hasidic worship. According to Hasidism, it is also possible to achieve devekut in daily activities, including eating, drinking, business affairs, and sex. Such ordinary acts become religious if in performing them one cleaves to God, and devekut is thus attainable by all Jews rather than merely a scholarly elite. Another feature of this movement is the zaddik, a spiritually elevated individual who is able to achieve the highest level of spiritual insight.

By the end of the eighteenth century, Hasidism had attracted numerous followers. The movement subsequently divided into a number of separate groups under different leaders, who passed on positions of authority to their descendants. Today, there are Hasidic communities in the United States, Israel and elsewhere. Like the Orthodox, they accept the fundamental religious beliefs of the tradition and strictly follow Jewish law. Throughout the Jewish world they are regarded with respect, and constitute an important and distinctive segment of the Jewish community.

The Baal Shem Tov

The Baal Shem Tov taught that sincere devotion to God is to be valued above traditional rabbinic learning:

> The Baal Shem Tov used to say: No child is born except as the result of joy and pleasure. In the same way, if a man wants his prayers to be heard, he must offer them up with joy and pleasure.

> The Baal Shem Tov used to say: Do not laugh at a man who gestures as he prays fervently. He gestures in order to keep himself from distracting thoughts which intrude upon him and threaten to drown his prayer. You would not laugh at a drowning man who gestures in the water in order to save himself.

> The Baal Shem Tov used to say: Sometimes a man becomes intoxicated with ecstasy when rejoicing over the law. He feels the love of God burning within him and the words of prayer come rushing out of his mouth. He must pray quickly to keep pace with them all.[3]

---

4. Conservative Judaism

The founder of what became known as Conservative Judaism was Zecharias Frankel. A supporter of moderate reform, he left the Reform rabbinical conference in Frankfurt in 1845 because the majority of participants had voted that there was no need to use Hebrew in the Jewish worship service. In Frankel's view, Judaism must be understood as a historically evolving dynamic religion. The aim of such an approach, he believed, would be to uncover the origins of the Jewish national spirit and its collective will.

In the United States a similar approach was adopted by a number of leading Jewish thinkers, including the Jewish scholar Solomon Schechter. In their view, Conservative Judaism should combine elements of both traditional and non-traditional Judaism. In February 1913 a union of 22 congregations was founded, committed to maintaining the Jewish tradition in its historical continuity. As the movement expanded in the 1920s and 30s, a degree of uniformity developed in congregational worship.

Conservative Jews view Judaism as an evolving historical organism that remains spiritually vibrant by adjusting to environmental and cultural conditions. As a result, Conservative thinkers sought to preserve those elements of the tradition which they believed to be spiritually meaningful, while setting aside those observances that actually hinder the continued growth of Judaism. In contrast with Orthodoxy, Conservative Jews feel no compulsion to accept theological doctrines that they believe to be outmoded.

In its quest to modernize the faith, Conservative scholars established an authoritative body to adapt Judaism to contemporary circumstances. As early as 1918 there was a considerable desire to create a body learned in the law, which would be able to advise the movement concerning pressing contemporary issues. Today, Conservative Judaism constitutes a major religious denomination within the Jewish world with its own rabbinical seminary, the Jewish Theological Seminary, in New York City.

Zecharias Frankel

Zecharias Frankel left the Reform Synod at Frankfurt because of the radical stance adopted by its participants. In his view, a less revolutionary approach should be adopted by reformers:

> Maintaining the integrity of Judaism simultaneously with progress, this is the essential problem of the present. Can we deny the difficulty of a satisfactory solution? Where is the point where the two apparent contraries can meet? … In order to have a conception of what changes should and can be introduced, we must ask ourselves the question – does Judaism allow any changes in any of its religious forms? Does it consider all of them immutable, or can they be altered? …

> We have then reached a decisive point in regard to moderate
> changes, namely, that they must come from the people and that
> the will of the entire community must decide ... The scholars
> thus have an important duty to make their work effective. It is
> to guard the sense of piety of the people and to raise their spirit
> to the height of the great ideas. For this they need the confidence
> of the people ... The truths of faith must be brought nearer to
> the people so that they may learn to understand the divine
> content within them and thus come to understand the spiritual
> nature and inner worth of the forms which embody these truths.[4]

5. Reconstructionist Judaism

The Reconstructionist movement emerged in the first half of the twentieth century in the United States under the influence of Mordecai Kaplan, Professor of Homiletics at the Jewish Theological Seminary. In his book *Judaism as a Civilization*, Kaplan argued that Judaism must be understood as an evolving civilization. In Kaplan's view, religion is the concretization of the self-consciousness of a group, which is manifest in spiritual symbols, places, events and writings. These symbols, he believed, inspire feelings of reverence, commemorate what the group believes to be most valuable, and provide historical continuity. In order for Judaism to survive, these elements of the tradition must be preserved.

Yet, Kaplan maintained that Judaism must divest itself of supernatural belief. The spiritual dimensions of the faith must be reformulated in humanistic and naturalistic terms. For Kaplan, God is not a supernatural being; rather God is 'trans-natural', 'super-factual', and super-experiential'. Departing from tradition, Kaplan maintained that God does not infringe on the law of nature. He is not the creator and sustainer of the universe who chose the Jewish people and guides their destiny. Many of these ideas were reflected in the movement's religious literature. *The New Haggadah for Passover*, for example, applied Kaplan's theology to liturgical texts, subordinating miracles and plagues to the narrative of Israel's redemption from Egypt.

In the 1940s and 50s the leaders of Reconstructionist Judaism insisted that they were not attempting to form a new branch of Judaism. Throughout this period, Reconstructionists hoped to influence the major Jewish denominations. Yet, by the end of the 1960s, the movement had itself become a denomination – it had created a seminary to train

Reconstructionist rabbis and had instituted a congregational structure. Today, in the United States, the movement has become a significant force on the Jewish scene.

Havurah

As an offshoot of Conservative Judaism, Reconstructionist Judaism is a relatively new movement – it is traditional in observance, but non-theistic in orientation. Many Reconstructionist congregations are composed of havurah groups united into a Federation. As the lay leader of one such congregation remarked:

> At this point we have approximately 200 households divided into about sixteen havurahs. We have group events as well as High Holy Day services. We also have a religious school which has about sixty-five kids. That happens every Sunday plus there is a Wednesday programme for Hebrew school. Typically we have Friday night services once a month and one havurah organizes the programming … These havurahs range from four or five families up to, in some instances, fourteen and fifteen families. They meet in each other's homes. What do they do? They all do a variety of different things, from scholarly discussions to life-cycle events to Sabbath dinners to picnics.[5]

---

6. Reform Judaism

As we have seen, Reform Judaism emerged at the beginning of the nineteenth century in opposition to Orthodoxy. In 1885 a gathering of Reform rabbis met in Pittsburgh, Pennsylvania to adopt a programme of reform. As we noted in Chapter 2, the Pittsburgh Platform insisted on a number of central principles of this new movement. According to these reformers, Judaism presents the highest conception of the God-idea as taught in holy Scriptures and developed and spiritualized by Jewish teachers. The Bible, they believed, is the record of the consecration of the Jewish people to its divine mission, yet it should be subject to scientific research. The Mosaic legislation, they declared, is a system of training the Jewish people, but today only the moral laws are binding. Rabbinic legislation is apt to obstruct rather than further modern spiritual elevation.

Further, the reformers rejected the belief in the Messiah as well as the doctrine of Heaven and Hell. It is the duty of modern Jews, they maintained, to strive for justice in modern society.

During the latter half of the nineteenth century the major institutions of Reform Judaism were established: the Central Conference of American Rabbis, the Hebrew Union College, and the Union of American Hebrew Congregations. As time passed, Reform Judaism became one of the three major Jewish religious denominations, with adherents throughout the United States, the diaspora and Israel.

Fifty years after the Pittsburgh meeting of 1885, the Jewish world had undergone major change. America was the centre of the diaspora; Zionism had become a vital force in Jewish life; the Nazis were in power in Germany. The Columbus Platform of the Reform movement adopted in 1937 reflected a new approach to liberal Judaism. In later years the Reform movement underwent further change. In the 1960s new liturgies were used, and in the 1970s a new Reform prayer book was published, which changed the content as well as the format of worship. In 1972 the first woman rabbi was ordained, and by the early 1980s more than seventy-five women had entered the rabbinate. In 1976 the Reform movement produced the San Francisco Platform – the purpose of this statement was to provide a unifying document that would bring a sense of order to the movement. More recently, a further platform was issued by the Central Conference of American Rabbis.

Abraham Geiger

In the middle of the nineteenth century, Abraham Geiger was one of the leaders of Reform Judaism. Here he argues that modern Jews must adopt a more critical approach to the Bible and the Talmud:

The Talmud and the Bible, too, that collection of books, most of them so splendid and uplifting, perhaps the most exalting of the literature of human authorship, can no longer be viewed as of Divine origin. Of course, all this will not come to pass today, or even tomorrow, but it should be our goal, and will continue to be so, and in this fashion we are working closely with every true endeavour and movement of our day, and we will accomplish more by study than we could by means of a hundred sermons and widespread religious instruction. For the love of Heaven, how much longer can we continue this deceit, to expound the stories of the Bible from the pulpits over and over again as actual historical happenings, to accept as supernatural events of world import stories which we ourselves have relegated to the realm of legend, and to derive our teachings from them or, at least, to use them as the basis for sermons and texts? How much longer will we continue to pervert the spirit of the child with these tales that distort the natural good sense of tender youth?[6]

7. Humanistic Judaism

Like Reconstructionist Judaism, Humanistic Judaism offers a non-supernatural interpretation of the Jewish faith. Originating in the 1960s in Detroit, Michigan under the leadership of Sherwin Wine who had been ordained as a Reform rabbi at the Hebrew Union College, Humanistic Judaism now numbers about 40,000 members in the United States, Israel and elsewhere. The movement originated in 1965 when the Birmingham Temple in a suburb outside of Detroit began to publicize its philosophy of Judaism. Later, two new congregations were created in Illinois and Connecticut. In 1969 the Society for Humanistic Judaism was established in Detroit to provide a basis for cooperation among Humanistic Jews, and in 1970 the first annual conference of the Society took place. During the next ten years, other congregations were established throughout the United States. In later years, Secular Humanistic Judaism became an international movement.

In the mid-1980s the movement proclaimed its ideology and aims. In a policy statement, it asserted that Humanistic Jews value human reason and the reality of the world that reason discloses. According to Humanistic Judaism, the natural universe stands on its own, requiring no supernatural intervention. In this light, Humanists believe in the value of human existence and in the power of human beings to solve their problems individually and collectively. Life, they maintain, should be directed to the satisfaction of human needs. In their view, Judaism is a human creation: it embraces all manifestations of Jewish life, including Jewish languages, ethical traditions, historic memories, cultural heritage, and especially the emergence of the State of Israel in modern times.

The Jewish people, Humanists insist, is a world with a pluralistic culture and civilization all its own. Judaism, as the culture of the Jews, has more than theological content. It encompasses many languages, a vast body of literature, historical memories, and ethical values. Yet, unlike other modern movements, Humanistic Judaism seeks to welcome all people who wish to identify with Jewish culture and destiny. Hence, Humanists have redefined the definition of Jewishness. A Jew, they state, is a person of Jewish descent or any person who declares him or herself to be a Jew and who identifies with the history, ethical values, culture, civilization, community and faith of the Jewish nation.

Humanistic Judaism offers an option for those Jews who wish to identify with the Jewish community despite their rejection of the traditional understanding of God's nature and activity. Unlike Reconstructionist Judaism, with its emphasis on the observances of the past, Humanistic Judaism fosters a radically new approach. The Jewish heritage is relevant only in so far as it advances Humanistic ideals. In addition, traditional definitions and principles are set aside in the quest to create a Judaism consonant with a scientific and pluralistic age.

Humanistic Celebrations

In accord with Humanistic ideology, traditional Jewish festivals are reinterpreted in a non-theistic fashion. The Sabbath, for example, is viewed as a time for Jewish renewal:

Shabbat (Sabbath) offers opportunities for both home and community ceremonies: candlelighting, wine and the eating of braided bread (hallah), with blessings that express human power and responsibility. Shabbat celebrations for Humanistic Jews are tributes to Jewish solidarity, to the shared Jewish past, present, and future. They provide opportunities to learn about, articulate, discuss and celebrate Humanistic and Jewish history, philosophy and values. Humanistic Shabbat celebrations recognize the individual's connections to humanity: a family, a community, a nation, the world.[7]

---

8. Jewish Buddhists

The members of the Jewish Buddhist movement (known as JuBus or BuJus) seek to combine their Jewish background with practices drawn from the Buddhist tradition. The term JuBu was first brought into circulation with the publication of *The Jew in the Lotus* by Roger Kamenetz. On a journey with a small group of Jewish leaders and rabbis, he met the Dalai Lama, the leader of Tibetan Buddhism, who had been exiled from Tibet by the Chinese regime. *The Jew in the Lotus* emerged from this expedition and explores Kamenetz's reflections on his own Jewishness and the attraction of Buddhism.

For Kamenetz and others, Jewish Buddhism offers a means to a journey into a deeper spirituality by blending together various elements of both faiths. For JuBus, the Buddhist tradition provides a means of entry into the religious treasures of their own faith. As members of this movement are keen to point out, both Judaism and Buddhism contain a number of common practices: they both emphasize acting ethically; each is based on a body of teachings passed on for thousands of years; each teaches respect for spiritual leaders; both stress that actions have consequences, but that errors can be atoned for and purified; neither group proselytizes, though both accept newcomers; Jews and Buddhists alike treat their texts and holy objects with veneration; and, significantly, some of their mystical teachings are similar.

JuBus argue that immersion into Buddhism can serve to help Jews to discover their Jewish roots. The Jewish history of persecution and displacement, for example, is echoed by the treatment of Tibetan Buddhists at the hands of the Chinese. Both Moses and Buddha had life-changing experiences that caused them to flee the royal court. There is also similarity between the tree of life in Genesis and the Bodhi tree under which the Buddha was first enlightened. JuBus further point out that both traditions encourage questioning and debate. Despite the icons and statutes associated with Buddhism, both religions reject images and forms of the Ultimate, conceiving the Absolute to transcend all form and limitation.

JuBu Spirituality

A commentator on the mix of Judaism and Buddhism, describes the attractions of such blending of traditions:

> No one knows for certain how many JuBus there are; the last surveys were conducted in the 1970s. Most of the three million Buddhists in the United States are Asian, but perhaps 30 per cent of all newcomers to Buddhism are Jewish.
>   Alan Lew, who studied Buddhism for a decade before changing courses to become a rabbi, calls the paradoxical blend

of Judaism, which bows to one God, and Buddhism, which has no supreme being, 'a fruitful and beautiful meeting of two religious systems that came together in the United States …'

A majority of JuBus, as they call themselves, are Baby Boomers who were raised in loosely religious families and began to feel unfulfilled in the tumultuous 1960s and l970s. They joined the legions of other young men and women searching for spiritual nourishment, and ended up turning to Buddhism, a welcoming meditative practice devoid of the cultural stigmas contained in, say, Christianity or Islam.[8]

9. Messianic Jews

In the last few decades, Messianic Judaism emerged as a controversial movement on the religious scene. Although rejected by all groups across the Jewish spectrum, Messianic Jews (whom other Jewish movements regard as Christians) claim they are loyal to the tradition. In the 1970s a number of American Jewish converts to Christianity, known as Hebrew Christians, were committed to a church-based conception of Hebrew Christianity. Yet, at the same time, there emerged a growing segment of the Hebrew Christian community that sought a more Jewish lifestyle. Eventually, a division emerged between those who wished to identify as Jews and those who sought to pursue Hebrew Christian goals. The advocates of change attempted to persuade older members of the need to embrace Jewish values, yet the latter remained unconvinced. In time, the name of the movement was changed to Messianic Judaism.

Messianic Jews subscribe to the belief that Yeshua (Jesus) is the long-awaited Messiah. In this respect, Messianic Judaism and the earlier Hebrew Christian movement are based on the same belief system. Nonetheless, Messianic Jews are anxious to point out that there are important distinctions between their views and those of Hebrew Christians. A Hebrew Christian is an individual who sees himself as of Jewish origin and may desire to affirm his background. But, at the same time, he views himself as coming into the New Covenant. The Old Covenant has passed away, and as a result the practice of anything Jewish is contrary to his being part of the new people of God and body of Christ. Messianic Jews, on the other hand, believe that the Jew is still called by God.

Messianic Jews see themselves as the true heirs of the early disciples of the risen Lord. Anxious to identify with the Jewish nation, they seek to observe the central biblical festivals. Similarly, the various customs regulating the life cycle and lifestyle of Jews in biblical times remain binding. Messianic believers are thus united in their loyalty to the Jewish heritage as enshrined in Scripture. However, Messianic Jews are not legalistic in their approach to Judaism. Traditional observance is tempered with the desire to allow the Holy Spirit to permeate the Messianic community and animate believers in their quest to serve the Lord.

Hebrew Christians and Messianic Jews

According to one of the leaders of the movement, Paul Liberman, there is a fundamental distinction between being a Hebrew Christian and a Messianic Jew:

To some people there is no distinction between being a Messianic Jew and a Hebrew Christian. I think that I see one … The distinction comes bottom line down to the issue of congregational worship … The Hebrew Christian typically believes that a Messianic congregation is an option, it is no better and no worse than any other option, and (he) says that it is the same to go to a Christian denomination as it is to go to a Messianic congregation … Messianic Jews believe more strongly in the call (particularly of the Abrahamic covenant) to remain Jews and as a practical matter they have come to recognize that history has reflected that within ten years and certainly by a second generation there is an assimilation whereby Jews are no longer identified as Jews and there are practically no third generation Jewish believers who recognize their Jewish heritage. Messianic Jews commonly believe that as a practical matter this just does not work out and is not consistent with the call of the Abrahamic covenant and elsewhere to observe God's pattern of Jews being preserved.[9]

---

10. Jewish Renewal

Jewish Renewal brings together kabbalistic and Hasidic theory and practice into a non-Orthodox egalitarian framework. The movement has its origins in the North American counterculture of the late 1960s and early 1970s.

During this period, a number of young rabbis, academics and political activists established fellowships (havurot) for prayer and study in a reaction to what they perceived as the overly structured institutional organizations of mainstream Judaism. Initially, their main inspiration was the pietistic fellowship of the Pharisees and early Jewish sects; in addition, some of these groups attempted to function as fully fledged communes. Others formed communities in urban and suburban contexts.

Even though the early founders of Jewish Renewal consisted largely of men, American Jewish feminists were later actively involved. Initially, Jewish Renewal attracted little attention despite considerable publicity. However, with the publication of *The Jewish Catalogue, a Do-It-Yourself Judaism Kit*, more attention was focused on this emerging movement. By the 1980s a number of havurot moved away from traditional patterns of Jewish worship as members added English readings, chants, poetry and other elements from various spiritual traditions.

Pre-eminent among leaders of Jewish Renewal was Zalman Schachter-Shalomi, a Hasidic-trained rabbi who was ordained in the Lubavitch movement. In the 1960s he broke with Orthodox Judaism and founded his own organization, The B'nai Or Religious Fellowship. After the first national conference in 1985, the name B'nai Or was changed to P'nai Or to reflect the more egalitarian nature of the movement. Together with Arthur Waskow, Schachter-Shalomi broadened the focus of the organization. In 1993 it merged with the Shalom Centre to become ALEPH (Alliance for Jewish Renewal). This body served as the overarching association for like-minded havurot. Later, the movement became institutionalized in the form of the administrative ALEPH, the rabbinical association OhaLaH, and a formalized rabbinic ordination programme.

Statistical information about the number of Jews who affiliate with Jewish Renewal is not available. Nonetheless, the movement has had a profound impact on various non-Orthodox streams of Judaism within the United States. Arguably the greatest impact has been on Reconstructionist Judaism. In addition, Jewish Renewal has influenced other non-Orthodox movements in terms of the increased leadership roles of women, the acceptance of gays and lesbians, and liberal political activism.

Jewish Renewal

Jewish Renewal as a countercultural movement within the Jewish world seeks to reinvigorate the tradition:

The term Jewish Renewal describes a set of practices within Judaism that attempt to reinvigorate what it views as a moribund and uninspiring Judaism with mystical, Hasidic, musical and meditative practices drawn from a variety of traditional and untraditional, Jewish and other sources. In this sense, Jewish renewal is an approach to Judaism that can be found within segments of any of the Jewish denominations. The term also refers to an emerging Jewish movement, the Jewish Renewal Movement, which describes itself as a world-wide, transdenominational movement grounded in Judaism's prophetic and mystical traditions.[10]

11. Jewish Kabbalists

In contemporary society the kabbalistic tradition has served as a rich spiritual resource for an increasing number of Jews. In their quest to attain enlightenment, these religious seekers have embraced the teachings of modern kabbalists. Pre-eminent among contemporary Jewish mystics, Rav Philip Berg has drawn millions of Jews to the kabbalistic tradition through the creation of Kabbalah Centres throughout the Jewish world. Trained in traditional yeshivot, Rav Berg was deeply influenced by Rabbi Yehuda Brandwein, a student of Yehuda Ashlag, a kabbalistic scholar living in Palestine in the 1920s. As a devoted student of Brandwein, Berg was determined to spread the wisdom of kabbalah to a younger generation.

Of central importance in the kabbalistic system propounded by Ashlag, as expounded by Brandwein, is the Desire to Share. This, he argued, should replace the Desire to Receive. According to Brandwein, human beings have been given the gift of the Desire to Receive; this can be understood as an unusually large spiritual vessel containing divine light. Yet, it is a mixed blessing. Although it allows them to be persons filled with light, it can block them from true goodness. If individuals cannot transform their Desire to Receive into a Desire to Share, this will have the most negative results. The Desire to Receive will grow larger and larger until it swallows everything around it.

Developing Brandwein's views, Berg explained how spiritual growth is possible. Our souls, he asserted, are created for one reason only: the Desire to Share. But, when the Creator existed alone, sharing could not occur. There were no vessels to hold the endless light pouring out of him. So with nothing more than desire, he created those vessels which are our souls. Initially, these created souls received the divine light with no motive other than to receive for themselves alone. But as they were filled, a new yearning evolved – one that put them on a collision course with the Creator. Suddenly, in emulation of God, our souls developed a Desire to Receive for the purpose of sharing. But they were faced with the same dilemma as that which faced the Creator himself before he created the vessels. With every soul filled, there was no one and nothing with whom to share.

Thus, what Berg referred to as the 'Bread of Shame' came into being. This was shame at receiving so much and giving nothing in return. Shame at being in a position in which the soul had no opportunity to say yes or no to the Creator, and, by that exercise of will, prove itself worthy to receive and thus dispel the shame. The shame led to rebellion – mass rejection of the Creator's beneficence. When that happened, the light was withdrawn, darkness and the unclean worlds were created, and all became finite, or limited, and thus in need of receiving. With those worlds came the clay bodies – vessels desiring only to receive for themselves alone – in which our souls reside. Here they forever struggle against body energy, to share. For the modern kabbalist, this quest to eliminate the 'Bread of Shame' by sharing with others is the fundamental spiritual goal.

Kabbalah for the Layman

In *Kabbalah for the Layman*, Rav Berg explains that there is a fundamental distinction between kabbalah and science:

> Contemporary scientific thought and writing on the subject of the scientific method shows clearly that it is not the all-powerful tool that was once hoped. Perception, psychologists have finally realized, is an active process of sorting and interpreting, and not the passive, 'objective' absorption of stimuli implied by the scientific method. We must, in other words, have a priori knowledge – a concept that comes very close to the idea of faith – before we can see and understand. In the kabbalah, there is no rigid distinction between physical and spiritual forms, and the picture presented is one of a total, unified, interrelated system ... Science asks only how something exists within the dimensions or limitations of time, space, motion and causality; kabbalah goes further and confronts the question of why things exist at all.[11]

12. Jewish Feminists

The Jewish feminist movement seeks to improve the status of women within Judaism and to open up new opportunities for religious experience and leadership. Jewish feminism was spurred by a grassroots development that took place in the 1970s. A decade previously many Jewish women participated in the second wave of American feminism. At that time most of these women did not link their feminism to their religious or ethnic identification. However, eventually some women whose Jewishness was central to their self-understanding applied feminist insights to their condition as American Jewish women. Faced with a male religious establishment, they envisaged a new form of Jewish life that embraced women's concerns.

Initially, a small group of feminists, calling themselves Ezrat Nashim, associated with the New York Havurah, a countercultural fellowship and took the issue of equality of women to the 1972 convention of the Conservative Rabbinical Assembly. In meetings with rabbis and their wives, members of Ezrat Nashim called for a change in the status of Jewish women. In their view, women should have equal access with men in occupying public roles of status and honour in the Jewish community. The group focused on eliminating the subordination of women by equalizing their rights in marriage and divorce laws, the study of sacred texts, including women in the minyan (quorum necessary for communal prayer), and providing opportunities for women to assume positions of leadership in the synagogue as rabbis and cantors.

In the following year, secular and religious Jewish feminists under the auspices of the North American Jewish Student's Network convened a conference in New York City. They subsequently brought their message to a wider audience through various publications. Through their efforts Jewish feminists gained increasing support. Innovations, such as baby-naming ceremonies, feminist Passover seders, and ritual celebrations of the New Moon were introduced into communal settings in the home or synagogues. In the Reform movement, the principle of equality between the sexes became a cardinal principle. Similarly, within the Reconstructionist movement women were granted equal status. In time the Conservative movement also accepted the principle of equality. Within Orthodox Judaism, feminists also pressed for change, and a small number of Orthodox feminists established women's prayer groups that respected halakhic restraints on the role of women in Jewish life. Even though the Orthodox leadership deny feminists claims that women are accorded secondary status within traditional Judaism, Jewish feminism has had an impact on American Orthodoxy. Girls nowadays are provided with a more comprehensive education in Orthodox schools and Orthodoxy has embraced such rituals as celebrating the birth of a daughter and bat mitzvah rites.

Jewish Feminism

Despite the advances made by Jewish feminism, some Jewish women remain sceptical concerning the possibilities for radical change. As one Jewish feminist commented, it is difficult to overcome the inherent sexual bias of the tradition:

> Obviously Judaism is a patriarchal religion; obviously it's institutionalized sexism. It's role-based; it's gender-based. As far as feminists go, I have so much experience of women starting off exploring their Judaism and ending up being goddess worshippers. I've seen this trend a lot. I went to this fascinating lecture by someone called Starhawk, who's written several books. She was born Jewish, and she said in her talk that she's having a great time; she's banging a drum; she's the centre of her life.[12]

---

13. Jewish Vegetarians and Ecologists

Jewish vegetarianism is both a philosophy and lifestyle based on Jewish theology. In the modern world a growing number of Jews from across the religious spectrum have adopted vegetarianism as an authentic expression of Jewish values. According to Rabbi Abraham Isaac Kook, the first chief rabbi of Israel, vegetarianism is the ideal, symbolizing the ultimate peace between human beings and the animal kingdom. In his view, in the Messianic Age as prophesied in the Book of Isaiah everyone will adopt a vegetarian diet. The only sacrifices that will be offered in the Temple will be the minhah sacrifice, which is of vegetable origin. This view is based on the ethical concept of tsaar baalei hayyim (preventing the suffering of living creatures), a principle extolled in biblical and rabbinic sources. Later rabbinic codes of law enshrine the notion of tsaar baalei hayyim as an important feature of the faith.

As an extension of the concern with animal welfare, many Jewish vegetarians also focus on the significance of numerous environmental threats. Acid rain, global warming, ozone layer depletion, erosion of topsoil, destruction of forests and other environments, pollution of water and soil, and toxic waste pose fundamental problems in the modern world. Given that Judaism teaches that the earth is the Lord's and that we are to be partners and co-workers with God in protecting the environment, Jews have ecological responsibilities for the planet. Hence, it is vital that Jewish values be applied towards the solution of these pressing problems.

Jewish Ecology

Jewish ecologists stress the need for human beings to protect the environment in a technological age:

> Before we can hope to solve the problems of ecology in the technological age, we must get at the roots of these problems. These lie primarily in our basic attitude toward the purpose of our life – in our choice of priorities, in the secular society, the top priority is self-interest. Any sense of responsibility toward the world at large is – if it exists at all – extremely secondary ...
>
> The Torah attacks this problem by helping us to change our inner motivation. Specifically, The whole of Torah is for the sake of social harmony ... The Torah shapes the human personality on two planes. It works on the cognitive level by providing a rational and integrated ideology and world view conducive to social harmony. It works along behaviourist lines by imposing a body of regulations prescribing in detail the required course of action in given situations. By developing an awareness of the divine origin of the prescribed code of conduct of Jewish law, it nurtures inner motivation and thus minimizes the need for externally imposed enforcement and the concomitant bureaucracy. The Torah views man as being entrusted with the orderly and proper management of the world. Therefore we may not stand aside and watch the world being destroyed.[13]

14. Gay and Lesbian Jews

Within the Jewish world there is a substantial number of gay and lesbian Jews. In North America alone it is estimated that about 500,000 members of the larger Jewish community are gay or lesbian. The various movements within Judaism differ in their view of homosexuality. According to the Bible, homosexual acts are an abomination. Thus Leviticus 18:22 states: 'And you shall not cohabit with a male as one cohabits with a woman; it is an abomination.' Again, Leviticus 20:13 declares: 'And if a man cohabits with a male as with a woman, both of them have done an abominable thing. They shall be put to death.' On the basis of such teaching, homosexuality is forbidden within Orthodox Judaism.

The more liberal branches, however, have embraced both gays and lesbians. Conservative Judaism, for example, did not allow for the ordination of openly gay men and women for over one hundred years. In addition, Conservative rabbis who performed same-sex commitment ceremonies did so without the Law Committee's sanction. Yet on 6 December 2006 the Committee on Jewish Law and Standards (CJLS) of the Rabbinical Assembly decreed that Conservative rabbis, synagogues and institutions can perform or host same-sex commitment ceremonies and are free to hire openly gay rabbis and cantors if they so wish. The decisions of the CJLS are only advisory, yet this body does represent the movement as a whole.

More liberal in its outlook, the Reform movement actively supports the rights of gays and lesbians. Over the last 15 years the Union of American Hebrew Congregations (UAHC) admitted to membership four synagogues with an outreach to gay and lesbian Jews. Hundreds of men and women who previously felt alienated from Judaism have joined these synagogues and added their strength to the Jewish community. In 1977 the UAHC called for an end to discrimination against homosexuals and expanded upon this in 1987 by calling for full inclusion of gay and lesbian Jews in all aspects of synagogue life. Subsequently, the movement has embarked on a programme of heightened awareness and education to achieve the fuller acceptance of gay and lesbian Jews.

World Congress of Gay, Lesbian, Bisexual and Transgender Jews

Today the movement for the acceptance of gay and lesbian Jews has become a worldwide phenomenon:

The World Congress of Gay, Lesbian, Bisexual and Transgender Jews, Keshet Ga'avah, consists of more than 25 member organizations worldwide. The World Congress holds both regional and world conferences catering to the interests of lesbian, gay, bisexual and transgender Jews around the world. The Hebrew subtitle Keshet Ga'avah – Rainbow of Pride – emphasizes the importance of Hebrew and of Israel to the World Congress.

Since its establishment in 1975 The World Congress of Gay, Lesbian, Bisexual and Transgender Jews, Keshet Ga'avah, has held conferences all over the world. Our conferences have empowered both local and visiting GLBT Jews …

Our vision is an environment where Lesbian, Gay, Bisexual and Transgender (LGBT) Jews worldwide can enjoy free and fulfilling lives.

GOALS:
In support of our vision, our goals are:
- to be the worldwide voice of LGBT Jews;
- to support, inspire, and strengthen local groups;
- to foster a sense of community among diverse individuals and organizations;
- to achieve equality and security for LGBT members worldwide.

GUIDING PRINCIPLES:
To achieve our goals, we value:
- diversity among groups and individuals;
- self-determination and respect for the autonomy of local organizations and individuals;
- transparent organizational structure; and
- close ties between LGBT Israelis and LGBT Jews around the world.[14]

Chapter 5

Modern Challenges to Judaism

Through the centuries the Jewish people were sustained by a belief in an all-good and all-powerful God who revealed his will on Mount Sinai and exercised providence over all creatures. On the basis of such a commitment, the nation was united by a dedication to a shared religious tradition. Yet, as we have seen in a post-Enlightenment world, the Jewish community has fragmented into a number of subgroups with conflicting orientations and ideologies. The shattering of the monolithic system of Judaism has resulted from a variety of causes. First, it has become increasingly difficult to sustain the biblical and rabbinic picture of God in the light of scientific discovery. In addition, the events of the Holocaust have posed fundamental questions about the notion of a benevolent Deity who cares for his children as a loving father. Further, the findings of biblical scholarship have called into question the doctrine of Torah MiSinai (the belief that God gave the Torah to Moses on Mount Sinai). Under the impact of these developments, Jewish belief has undergone a process of disintegration: no longer is it possible for most Jews to believe in such doctrines as the coming of the Messiah, the resurrection of the dead, messianic redemption and final judgement, and there has been a growing disenchantment with religious observances. Jewry has ceased to be one people with a common heritage. Rather, the Jewish community has disintegrated into antagonistic factions that lack a shared religious vocabulary.

The Challenge to Theism

As we have seen, throughout history Jews have subscribed to a belief in an all-good, all-powerful and all-knowing God who created the universe, sustains it and guides humanity to its ultimate fulfilment in a world-to-come. Such belief sustained the Jewish people through suffering and tragedy and provided the nation with a sense of ultimate purpose. Since the Enlightenment, however, this religious conviction has been challenged in various ways, leading to the fragmentation of the monolithic religious system of the Jewish past. Arguably the most serious challenge to traditional Jewish belief has been the expansion of scientific investigation. Since the Renaissance, scientific knowledge has increased in such fields as astronomy, geology, zoology, chemistry and physics. Discoveries in these areas have called into question biblical claims about the origin and nature of the universe.

Increasingly, it has become clear that in giving an account of the history of the Jewish nation, the biblical writers relied on a pre-scientific understanding of the world. In the last few centuries, scholarly investigations into the culture of the ancient Near East have provided a basis for reconstructing the primitive worldview that provided the framework for the thinking of the ancient Israelites. As a result of the expansion of scientific knowledge and an increased awareness of the thought-world of biblical writers, most modern Jews are no longer able to accept the scriptural account of the origin and nature of the world as well as God's activity. The vast majority of Jews, for example, no longer find credible the biblical cosmology of a three-storied universe with heaven in the sky, hell beneath, and the sun circling around the earth. Further, most Jews have abandoned the belief that the world was created some six thousand years ago, and that human beings and animals came into being in their present forms at the same time. Again, the notion that at some future date the decomposed corpses of humanity will be resurrected no longer seems plausible in the light of a scientific understanding of the laws of nature. In essence, the modern age has witnessed scientific advance on the one hand, and the retreat of traditional belief on the other.

Science and the Bible

Reflecting on his Orthodox Jewish education, the manager of a restaurant in the United States commented:

I could not reconcile anything these people were talking about with anything that made any sense: miracles, prohibitions – keep the whole thing! There was one thing that set the seeds in motion very early on. I used to go to the Metropolis Science Museum. The folks took me; I went there all the time. I loved it. You see these prehistoric things, and all that stuff. When I learnt how to read, I see these things are sixty million years old. They got dates on 'em. How come then, in religion school, the calendar is 5,000 and some years old? So I start thinking about it. This was when I was about seven or eight. And I say, 'There's something wrong here. These people are telling me the world started 5,000 years ago and these things are sixty million years old.' So I go into the rabbi and I say, 'How come?' He says, 'That's the way it is.' And I say, 'How can you say that's the way it is? I'm reading the Bible already, and I don't see anything about dinosaurs in there. Somewhere, somebody's got something wrong. I don't know who, but somebody's got something wrong.' And all he keeps telling me is, 'That is what we believe in. Believe in it.' I say, 'Thank you,' and out I go.[1]

The climate of thought in the twenty-first century is thus one in which scientific explanation has taken over the role of theological interpretation. Even though the sciences have not disproved the claims of religion, they have provided a rational explanation of events that previously would have been understood as the result of God's will. In this light, faith has come to be regarded as a personal preoccupation that is destined to be ousted from the central areas of human knowledge until at last it will have the same status as such fields as astrology. In the future, religion is likely to be perceived as an antiquated relic of previous ages when scientific knowledge was less extensive. The sciences have thus effectively established the autonomy of the natural world.

A second objection to the traditional understanding of God and his action in the world is the fact of evil. For many, it is the existence of human suffering that makes the idea of a perfectly loving God utterly implausible. As a challenge to religious belief the problem of evil has traditionally been formulated as a dilemma: if God is perfectly loving, He must wish to abolish evil; and if He is all-powerful, He must be able to abolish evil. But evil exists: therefore God cannot be both omnipotent and perfectly loving. In a post-Holocaust world this religious perplexity has been highlighted by the terrors of the Nazi era. An illustration of the potency of this problem is elucidated by the Jewish writer, Elie Wiesel. In his autobiographical novel *Night* he depicted his transition from youthful belief to disillusionment. At the beginning of the novel the author described himself as a young boy fascinated with God's mystery, studying Talmud and kabbalah in the Transylvanian town of Sighet. Later, he was transported to Auschwitz where the erosion of his faith began. Shortly after his arrival, he questioned God: 'Some talked of God, of his mysterious ways, of the sins of the Jewish people and their future deliverance. But I had ceased to pray. How I sympathized with Job. I did not deny God's existence, but I doubted his absolute justice.'

In a short time his religious rebellion deepened. In particular he was shocked by the incongruity of the Jewish liturgy that praised God despite the events of the camps. Dismayed by the new arrivals who recited the kaddish prayer for the dead when they recognized the nature of their plight, he felt revolt rise within him. 'Why should I bless his name?' he asked. 'The Eternal, Lord of the Universe, the all-powerful and terrible was silent. What had I to thank him for?' As the novel continues, Wiesel's anger increased. At the New Year service, he refused to bless God and praise the universe in which there was mass murder: 'This day I had ceased to plead. I was no longer capable of lamentation. On the contrary, I felt very strong. I was the accuser, God the accused.' On Yom Kippur, he decided not to fast, 'There was no longer any reason why I should fast. I no longer accepted God's silence. As I swallowed my bowl of soup, I saw in the gesture an act. In the depths of my heart, I felt a great void.'

Many Jews have shared Wiesel's despair; no longer are they able to subscribe to a belief in an all-good, providential Deity who lovingly watches over his chosen people. Although a number of Jewish theologians have suggested solutions to this problem of suffering, none has provided an adequate answer. As we have noted in Chapter 3, the Orthodox theologian, Bernard Maza, for example, argued in *With Fury Poured Out* that God brought about the Holocaust so as to ensure that Torah Judaism would flourish in the modern world. In formulating this thesis Maza presupposed that God is an all-powerful, benevolent Lord of history who is concerned with the destiny of his people. However, if God was ultimately responsible for the horrors of the death camps, it seems impossible to reconcile such mass murder with the traditional concept of God's nature. Surely if God is all-good, He would have wished to rescue innocent Jewish victims from the hands of the Nazis. If He is omnipotent He would have the power to do so. Yet Maza contended that the Holocaust was an outpouring of God's fury. Surely, if God was concerned with the future of Torah Judaism, He could have accomplished his purposes without slaughtering a vast segment of the Jewish population.

Divine Providence and the Holocaust

In *With Fury Poured Out*, the Orthodox theologian Bernard Maza maintained that the Holocaust was part of God's providential plan for reinvigorating Torah Judaism:

> It was the will of Hashem (God) that the Jewish people, the bearers of the Torah, would not forsake the Torah.
> The present generation of righteous would not be the last. The ambition of the coming generation to be like all the nations of the world would not be.
> Hashem knew that the oppression of the Jewish people had to end or the sun of Torah would set. The Jewish people had to be redeemed and returned to the land of Israel. Only in the land of Israel would they find freedom from the suffering that was inevitably their lot in the lands of their exile ...
> This was therefore the moment in the divine history of the Jewish people that Hashem judged to be the time of redemption from oppression ... The prophet Ezekiel had said: 'As I live', says the Lord, 'that only with a strong hand and an outstretched arm, and with fury poured out will I be King over thee.'[2]

Like Maza, the Reform theologian Ignaz Maybaum believed that the Holocaust was the result of divine providence. But, as we observed in Chapter 3, in contrast to Maza, Maybaum argued in *The Face of God after Auschwitz* that God did not pour out his fury to revitalize Torah Judaism. Rather, Maybaum believed that six million Jews who died in the concentration camps were chosen by God to become sacrificial victims in order to bring about God's purposes for the modern world. Again, there are serious difficulties with such a view. First, it makes no sense to think that God entered into a covenantal relationship with the Jewish people to crucify them. Maybaum contended that, like Nebuchadnezzar, Hitler was an instrument of God, yet if God is omnipotent there would have been no need to murder six million Jews to inaugurate a new epoch in human history. While Maybaum appears to follow the doctrine of omnipotence to its seemingly logical conclusion (God must be the cause of the Holocaust, He did not defend his attributes of love and justice), for most Jews it is impossible to believe in a God who would be the source of the terrors of the death camps.

Divine Destruction

In *The Face of God and Auschwitz*, Ignaz Maybaum argues that the Holocaust was part of God's providential plan. In his view, Hitler served as a divine instrument:

> Thus Hitler came. He, the Nihilist, did what the progressives should have done but failed to do, he destroyed the Middle Ages, but did so by destroying the old Europe. The sins of a stagnant Europe, the sins of an isolationist America, the sins of the democracies, failing to progress towards the solution of the new problems gave birth to Hitler ... Would it shock you if I were to imitate the prophetic style and formulate the phrase: Hitler, my Servant?[3]

Like both Maza and Maybaum, the Jewish philosopher Emil Fackenheim offered a positive theological response to the Holocaust in a wide range of writings. In his view, as mentioned in Chapter 3, God issued a further commandment to his chosen people out of Auschwitz. This 614th commandment decrees that Jews are forbidden to hand Hitler posthumous victories – they are commanded to survive as Jews, lest the Jewish people perish. The central difficulty with this position is that Fackenheim failed to give a justification for this claim; for those individuals who find it difficult to believe in God after the Holocaust, he did not provide an explanation for his conviction that God was present at Auschwitz and is providentially concerned with the destiny of his chosen people.

Such attempts to provide an explanation of God's ways have not persuaded most Jews whose faith has been shaken by the events of the Nazi era. In contemporary society traditional religious belief in God has been eclipsed by an overwhelming sense that the universe is devoid of a divine presence. For many, the views of the radical Jewish theologian, Richard Rubenstein, reflect their predicament. In *After Auschwitz*, as referred to in Chapter 3, Rubenstein declared that he was no longer able to accept the traditional biblical and rabbinic conception of God. 'When I say we believe in the time of the death of God,' he wrote, 'I mean that the thread uniting God and man, Heaven and earth, has been broken. We stand in a cold, silent, unfeeling cosmos, unaided by any powerful power beyond our own resources. After Auschwitz what else can a Jew say about God?'

 A third major challenge to Jewish theism stems from naturalistic interpretations of the origin of religion: sceptics assert that supernatural experience can be adequately accounted for without postulating the existence of God. Pre-eminent among these views is the sociological theory of religion postulated by such thinkers as Emile Durkheim. According to this theory, the gods whom human beings worship are imaginary – they are unconsciously fabricated by society as instruments whereby the thoughts and behaviour of individuals can be controlled. Even though the devout believe they are in the presence of a higher power that transcends their lives, they are in fact under an illusion. The reality they acknowledge is not a supernatural being; rather it is a symbol of society itself. God is thus simply a reflection of society's absolute claim upon the loyalty of its members. On this account, the religious practices of a particular group are rooted in the needs of the community. As social beings, men and women have conceived of society as an external reality invested with holiness. Here then, is an interpretation of religion that involves no reference to God as an external Deity who created and oversees human destiny.

For many Jews, such an understanding of religion has had considerable appeal. Mordecai Kaplan, the founder of Reconstructionist Judaism, for example, based his explanation of Judaism as a civilization on such an interpretation. Explaining the evolution of religious belief, he wrote in *Judaism as a Civilization*:

> Long before the human being was able to formulate the idea 'God', he was aware that there were elements in his environment, certain animate and inanimate objects, definite places, particular persons upon whose help he depended for the fulfilment of his needs. He ascribed to them power, which he believed he could direct to his advantage by resorting to actions and formulas which we term magic … As man developed further, he extended the domain of holiness to include not only visible or pictureable objects, events and persons, but also customs, laws, social relationships, truths and ideals.[4]

Within the Jewish world such a naturalistic interpretation of religious belief has gained a considerable following. Another naturalistic explanation of religion that has had a similar impact is psychological in character. Writers such as Sigmund Freud have contended that religious beliefs are nothing more that psychic defences against the threats of human existence. As Freud explained in *The Future of an Illusion*, nature rises up against us, majestic, cruel and inexorable. Yet human beings can employ methods to subdue such dangers:

> We can apply the same methods against these violent supermen outside that we employ in our own society; we can try to adjure them, to appease them, to bribe them and, by so influencing them, we may rob them of part of their power.[5]

In contemporary society there has been a growing acceptance of such a psychological explanation of religious belief. So these challenges to theism – stemming from the growth of science, the existence of human misery and suffering, and the emergence of naturalistic explanations of religious commitment – constitute major obstacles to traditional religious belief in the modern world.

Divine Revelation and Biblical Scholarship

According to traditional Judaism, the Five Books of Moses were dictated by God to Moses on Mount Sinai. This doctrine implies that the entire text – including precepts, theology and history – is of divine origin: all of its contents are inerrant. Such a belief guarantees the validity of the legal system, the Jewish view of God, and the concept of Israel's pre-eminence among the nations. In the modern period, however, it has become increasingly difficult to sustain this concept of Scripture in the light of scholarly investigation and discovery. As early as the sixteenth century, scholars pointed out that the Five Books of Moses appear to be composed of different sources. In the sixteenth century, Thomas Hobbes, in his *Leviathan*, accepted the Mosaic authorship of the Pentateuch but not of the anachronisms in the biblical text. In the same century, Baruch Spinoza in his *Tractatus Theologico-Politicus* asserted that the Pentateuch is a composite work compiled during the time of Ezra. Again, Richard Simon published a work at this time in which he argued that the Pentateuch is a compilation of documents of different dates. In his view, the commandments were inspired by God, but the biblical narrative is of human origin.

These studies were followed in the next century by the work of Jean Astruc, generally considered to be the founder of modern biblical criticism. In a work published in 1753, he noted that entire portions of Genesis use the divine name Elohim, whereas other portions use the Tetragrammaton, YHWH. This observation led Astruc to conjecture that one of the documents used by Moses was the Elohist (the document describing the origins of the universe). In Astruc's view there were 13 documents that Moses used in compiling the Torah. Later, other scholars, basing their interpretations on Astruc's work, maintained that various fragments of documents could be detected in the Torah, or that an original work of Moses had been expanded at different times. Eventually, scholars concluded that two major documents were used in the compilation of the Pentateuch: one using the divine name Elohim and the other the Tetragrammaton. At the beginning of the eighteenth century, De Wette published a work in which he claimed that Deuteronomy was compiled shortly before it was discovered in the time of Josiah.

In the middle of the nineteenth century, sustained investigation by Karl Heinrich Graf and Julius Wellhausen concluded that the Five Books of Moses were composed of four main documents, which once existed separately but were later combined by a series of editors or redactors. The first document, J, dating from the ninth century BCE, attributes the most anthropomorphic character to God, referred to by the four Hebrew letters YHWH. The second source, E, stemming from the eighth century BCE, is less anthropomorphic and utilizes the divine name Elohim. In the seventh century BCE, the D source was written, concentrating on religious purity and the priesthood. Finally, the P source from the fifth century BCE, which has a more transcendental view of God, emphasizes the importance of the sacrificial cult.

By utilizing this framework, Graf and Wellhausen maintained that it is possible to account for the manifold problems and discrepancies in the biblical text: for example, there are two creation accounts in Genesis; the appointment of a king is sanctioned in Deuteronomy, but opposed in 1 Samuel; Isaac appears to have spent eighty years on his deathbed; camels bearing loads are mentioned in the narratives even though they were not domesticated until much later; the centralization of worship in Deuteronomy was unknown in prophetic times. These are only a few illustrations of textual difficulties that can be resolved be seeing the Five Books of Moses as the result of the weaving together of source material from different periods in the history of ancient Israel.

The Graf–Wellhausen hypothesis was, however, modified by subsequent writers. Some scholars have preferred not to speak of separate sources but of circles of tradition. On this view, J, E, P and D represent oral traditions rather than written documents. These scholars stress further that the separate traditions themselves contain early material; thus it is a mistake to think they originated in their entirety at particular periods. Other scholars reject the theory of separate sources altogether; they argue that oral traditions were modified throughout the history of ancient Israel and only eventually were compiled into a single narrative. Yet, despite these different theories, there is a general recognition among biblical critics that the Torah was not written by Moses. Rather, it is seen as a collection of traditions originating at different times in ancient Israel.

Another major challenge to the traditional belief that God revealed the Torah to Moses on Mount Sinai stems from the field of biblical archaeology. From what is now known of Mesopotamian civilization, we can see that the Bible reflects various aspects of this cultural milieu. The physical structure of the universe as outlined in Genesis parallels what is found in Near Eastern literature: the earth is conceived as a thin disk floating in the surrounding waters; under the earth is the abode of the dead. Like the gods of ancient literatures, the God of Israel is understood anthropomorphically. As with other peoples, the Israelites accepted magical procedures (Exod. 7: 11, 12), recognized the power of blessings and curses (Numbers 22–4), and believed that God's will can be known through dreams, dice and oracles. Furthermore, as in other cultures, holy men, kings and priests were revered, and there was a preoccupation with ritual uncleanliness and purity as well as with priestly rites. In addition to these similarities, there are strong parallels between the Bible and the literature of the ancient Near East: Genesis appears to borrow details from the Mesopotamian *Epic of Gilgamesh* in connection with the legend of the flood; and biblical law bears a striking resemblance to ancient legal codes: for example, the Assyrian treaties between a king and his vassals is very like the covenantal relationship between God and Israel. Yet, despite these parallels, Israelite monotheism radically transformed such features: mythological themes, where retained in the Bible, are only briefly mentioned; biblical heroes are not worshipped; the underworld is never a subject for speculation; the cult is free of rites to placate ghosts and demons; there is no ancestor worship; divination (such as investigating the entrails of sacrificial animals) is forbidden. In essence, the biblical narratives are simplified and demythologized. There are no myths of the birth of gods, their rivalries, sexual relations or accounts of death and resurrection. Moreover, there is no mention of fate to which both men and gods are subject. Instead, the Bible concentrates on the moral condition of humanity within the context of divine providence.

Code of Hammurabi

The Code of Hammurabi was discovered in 1901. Hammurabi is believed to be the Amraphel referred to in Genesis 14:1; his date has been given as about 2130–2088 BCE. There are parallels between this Code and the laws of the ancient Israelites:

> If a physician operate on a man for a severe wound (or make a severe wound upon a man) with a bronze lancet and save the man's life; or if he open an abscess (in the eye) of a man with a bronze lancet and save that man's eye, he shall receive 10 shekels of silver (as his fee).

If he be a freeman, he shall receive 5 shekels.

If he be a man's slave, the owner of the slave shall give 2 shekels of silver to the physician.

If a physician operate on a man for a wound with a bronze lancet and cause the man's death; or open an abscess (in the eye) of a man with a bronze lancet and destroy this eye, they shall cut off his fingers.[6]

Such demythologization is a particular feature of the biblical narratives. According to modern scholarship, the priestly editors composed a creation account (Gen. 1:2–4) markedly different from the Babylonian narrative. In the *Enuma Elish*, which is a reworking of old Sumerian themes, the primordial power Tiamat (salt water) and Apsu (sweet water) gave birth to a pair of forces that engendered other gods such as Anu (the god of heaven) and Ea (the god of running waters). Apsu plotted the destruction of the gods but was prevented by Ea. Later, Tiamat, with a second husband and an army of gods and monsters, attacked the younger gods. Marduk (the god of Babylonia), however, slaughtered Tiamat and from her corpse fashioned the cosmos and from the blood of her consort Ea made man. Though there are echoes of this mythology in the Bible, Genesis declares that God formed the universe without any struggle against other gods. The enemies created by God's fiat have no divine aspect. Further, the abyss simply refers to the original state of the universe after a primary substance – an unformed and watery chaos – came into existence. Turning to the flood story – a central element of Mesopotamian myth – the Bible ignores such details as the gods' terror at the cataclysms accompanying the flood. In the Gilgamesh Epic, the flood is seen as the god Enil's remedy to reduce the level of human noise in the world. The Bible, however, proclaims that man's wickedness is its cause; and, after the flood, God imposed no laws to restrain future human evil, promising rather that such devastation will never happen again.

The Flood

A comparison of texts from the Babylonian flood story and the Bible forcefully illustrates the demythologizing intention of the biblical authors:

Gilgamesh Epic (eleventh canto)
I sent forth a dove and let her go,

But there was no resting place, and she returned.
Then I sent forth a raven and let her go,
The raven flew away, she beheld the abatement of the
waters,
And she came near, wading and croaking, but did not return.
Then I sent everything forth to the four quarters of heaven,
I offered sacrifice,
I made a libation on the peak of the mountain.
By sevens I sent out the vessels,
Under them I heaped up reed and cedarwood and myrtle,
The gods smelt the savour,
The gods gathered like flies about him that offered up the
sacrifice.

Genesis 8

Then he sent forth a dove from him, to see if the waters had subsided
from the face of the ground; but the dove found no place to set her
foot, and she returned to him ... He waited another seven days, and
sent forth the dove; and she did not return to him any more ... So,
Noah went forth, and his sons and his wife and his sons' wives with
him. And every beast, every creeping thing, and every bird, everything that moves upon the earth, went forth by families out of the
ark. Then Noah built an altar to the Lord, and took of every clean
animal and every clean bird, and offered burnt offerings on the altar.
And when the Lord smelled the pleasing odour, the Lord said in his
heart, 'I will never again curse the ground because of man, for the
imagination of man's heart is evil from his youth; neither will I ever
again destroy every living creature as I have done.'[7]

A final challenge to the traditional belief of Torah MiSinai is derived
from textual criticism. The assumption of Orthodoxy is that the text of
the Torah is the same as that revealed on Mount Sinai. This view suffers
from a number of difficulties. First, the Torah Scrolls used in the synagogue
are written in square script, yet in ancient times the Hebrew script was in
a different form as exhibited in the Gezer calendar (tenth century BCE),
the Moabite Stone (ninth century BCE), the Siloam inscription (eighth
century BCE), and the Lacish Letters (sixth century BCE). Thus, the
evidence of archaeology suggests that the Torah Scrolls must date from a
considerable time after the giving of the law on Mount Sinai and the
original form of the Five Books of Moses.

A more serious issue concerns the actual text of the Torah. The standard text was produced by the Masoretes, who flourished from the sixth to the ninth centuries. These textual scholars strove to produce an authoritative reading of the Bible. Consequently, they divided the biblical text into words and sentences as well as into segments of verse length, added vowel signs to the Hebrew words as well as cantillation marks indicating the articulation and inflections of the text for chanting, and indicated those cases where pronunciation or even the actual word used varied when the text is read aloud. Subsequently, the Masoretic Text was viewed as standard by Jewry. However, other texts suggest that the Masoretic Text does not conform to the original Torah.

The Dead Sea Scrolls from the second and first century BCE, for example, contain an early manuscript of the Book of Isaiah, the first two chapters of Habakkuk, and various other fragments. Even though the texts have a close affinity to those in the Masoretic Text, they contain a number of variants. Again, the Samaritan Pentateuch contains a number of alternative readings. Some of these variants appear to be a reworking of the original text in accordance with Samaritan doctrine; however, the Samaritan Pentateuch also contains nearly two thousand variant readings that are in accord with the Greek translation, the Septuagint, of the third century BCE. Thus these two early texts of the Bible may well more accurately mirror the original Hebrew than the Masoretic Text.

The Dissolution of Traditional Belief and Practice

Under the impact of modern science and contemporary secular trends, the system of traditional Jewish belief and practice has undergone a process of dissolution. As we have seen, many non-Orthodox Jews have abandoned various aspects of traditional Judaism. Regarding the concept of God, a number of Jewish thinkers have found it increasingly difficult to accept the fundamental tenets of the Jewish faith: some wish to modify various elements of Jewish theism, imposing limits to God's omnipotence or omniscience; others have sought a more radical solution, wishing to substitute the concept of a supernatural Deity in naturalistic terms. Mordecai Kaplan, for example, asserted that the idea of God must be redefined – the belief in a supernatural deity must be superseded by a concept of God as 'man's will to live'. At the far end of the religious spectrum, an even more radical approach has been advanced by Humanistic Jews who wish to dispense with God altogether. For these Jews, it is possible to live a Jewishly religious life without any acknowledgement of a divine reality. Thus, across the various groupings in contemporary Judaism there exists a wide range of different and conflicting beliefs about the nature of the Divine – no longer is the Jewish community committed to the view that God created and sustains the universe, guiding it to its ultimate fulfilment.

Redefining God

According to Mordecai Kaplan, the concept of God must be understood fundamentally in terms of its effect. Thus he wrote in 'The Meaning of God for the Contemporary Jew':

We learn more about God when we say that love is divine than when we say that God is love. A veritable transformation takes place ... Divinity becomes relevant to authentic experience and therefore takes on a definiteness which is accompanied by an awareness of authenticity ...

When religion speaks of salvation it means in essence the experience of the worthwhileness of life. When we analyse our present experience of life's worthwhileness we find that it is invariably based on specific ethical experiences – moral responsibility, honesty, loyalty, love, service. If carefully pursued, this analysis reveals that the source of our ethical experience is found in our willingness and ability to achieve self-fulfilment through reciprocity with others. This reciprocity in turn is an expression of a larger principle that operates in the cosmos in response to the demands of a cosmic force, the force that makes for creativity and interdependence in all things.[8]

Similarly, for many Jews, the traditional belief in Torah MiSinai no longer seems credible. The rabbinic understanding of Torah as revealed to Moses and infallibly transmitted through the sages has been undermined by the findings of modern scholarship. Thus, from the earliest period, reformers continued to belief in divine revelation, but they were anxious to point out that God's disclosure is mediated by human understanding. According to Reform Judaism, the Bible is a spiritual record of the history of ancient Israel, reflecting the primitive ideas of its own age. Similarly the Conservative movement views Scripture as historically conditioned and mediated through human apprehension. As the Jewish scholar Solomon

Schechter explained, the Torah is not in heaven – it is on earth and must be interpreted to be understood. For Reconstructionist Jews, the Torah is pre-eminently a human document, shaped by those who composed this epic account of Israel's origins and development. In this light, the Reconstructionist movement seeks to incorporate the Bible into the life of its members without ascribing to it a supernatural origin. Humanistic Jews as well share a similar veneration of the Torah even though they do not believe it was divinely revealed. Hence, as in the case of belief about God, there are fundamental differences of opinion regarding the status of Scripture among the various movements of contemporary Judaism.

Humanistic Judaism and Authority

Unlike Orthodox Judaism, which is based on the doctrine of Torah MiSinai, Humanistic Jews rely on reason as the most effective means of arriving at truth. As the *Guide to Humanistic Judaism* explains:

One of the most prominent characteristics of Jewish history is the vulnerability of Jews. Repeatedly, they learned a painful lesson: Do not trust your fortune to authority. At one moment it might promise safety and prosperity; in the next it might deliver violence and destruction ... the lesson of Jewish history remains valid: Do not trust external authority ... Thus do Humanism and Jewish experience confirm one another. Both demonstrate that (I) there is no authority in the universe, human or divine, that may rightfully impose its power on human beings; and (2) every person owns himself or herself and possesses the right to determine the purpose and course of his or her life.[9]

The doctrine of messianic redemption has likewise been radically modified within the various branches of non-Orthodox Judaism. In the earliest stage of development, reformers rejected the notion of a personal Messiah; instead they believed that the Messianic Age was beginning to dawn in their own time. In their view, history was evolving progressively towards an era of liberty, equality and justice for all people. Even though the events of the twentieth century have eclipsed these earlier messianic expectations, Reform Judaism still embraces the conviction that human progress is possible in the modern world. Similarly, many Zionists saw the founding of a Jewish homeland as the fulfilment of messianic hope. Rejecting the belief in a personal Messiah, they advocated a naturalistic interpretation of historical progress in which the Jewish people would be restored to the land of their ancestors. Such reinterpretations of traditional belief are indicative of the general shift away from supernaturalism in the modern world. As the Jewish theologian, Louis Jacobs, noted in *Principles of the Jewish Faith*: 'most modern Jews prefer to interpret the messianic hope in naturalistic terms, abandoning the belief in a personal Messiah, the restoration of a sacrificial system, and to a greater or lesser degree, the idea of direct divine intervention.'

The doctrine of the resurrection of the dead has likewise been largely rejected in both the Orthodox and non-Orthodox camps. The original belief in resurrection was an eschatological hope bound up with the rebirth of the nation in the Days of the Messiah, but as this messianic concept faded into the background so did this doctrine. For most Jews, physical resurrection is simply inconceivable in the light of the scientific understanding of the world. Thus, the Orthodox writer Joseph Seliger criticized the doctrine of resurrection as unduly materialistic. According to Seliger, in the ancient world the afterlife was depicted in terms of earthly existence. The Egyptians, for example, believed so strongly in the bodily aspect of the afterlife that they mummified the body and erected pyramids to protect it. In Seliger's view, such a notion is a mistaken folk-belief and has little in common with the law of Moses. Judaism, he maintained, does not, in fact, adhere to the belief in physical resurrection but to belief in the immortality of souls. In a similar vein, the former Chief Rabbi of the British Empire, J. H. Hertz, argued that what really matters is the doctrine of immorality. In his commentary on the Pentateuch he wrote:

Many and various are folk beliefs and poetical fancies in the rabbinical writings concerning Gan Eden (Heaven) and Gehinnom (Hell). Our most authoritative religious guides, however, proclaim that no eye hath seen, nor can mortal fathom, what awaiteth us in the Hereafter; but even the tarnished soul will not forever be denied spiritual bliss.[10]

In the Reform community a similar attitude prevails. As noted previously, the Pittsburgh Platform categorically rejected the doctrine of the soul, and such a conviction has been a dominant feature of the movement in subsequent years. Concerning Reform Jews, the Platform states:

We reassert the doctrine of Judaism that the soul is immortal, grounding this belief on the divine nature of the human spirit, which forever finds bliss in righteousness and misery in wickedness. We reject as ideas not rooted in Judaism the belief in bodily resurrection and in Gehenna and Eden (Hell and Paradise) as abodes for eternal punishment or reward.[11]

The point to note about the concept of the immortal soul in both Orthodox and non-Orthodox Judaism is that it is disassociated from traditional notions of messianic redemption and divine judgement.

Belief in eternal punishment has also been discarded by a large number of Jews, partly because of the interest in penal reform during the past century. Punishment as retaliation in a vindictive sense has been generally rejected. As Louis Jacobs remarked: 'the value of punishment as a deterrent and for the protection of society is widely recognized. But all the stress today is on the reformatory aspects of punishment. Against such a background the whole question of reward and punishment in the theological sphere is approached in a more questioning spirit.' Further, the rabbinic view of Hell is seen by many as morally repugnant. Jewish theologians have stressed that that it is a delusion to believe that a God of love could have created a place of eternal punishment. In his commentary on the prayer book, Chief Rabbi Hertz categorically declared: 'Judaism rejects the doctrine of eternal damnation'. And in *Jewish Theology*, the Reform theologian, Kaufmann Kohler, argued that the question of whether the tortures of Hell are reconcilable with divine mercy 'is for us superfluous and superseded. Our modern conception of time and space admits neither a place or a world-period for the reward and punishment of souls, nor the intolerable conception of eternal joy without useful action and eternal agony without any moral purpose.'

Traditional theological belief has thus lost its force for a large number of Jews in the modern period – no longer is it possible to discover a common core of religious belief underpinning Jewish life. The community instead is deeply divided on the most fundamental features of the Jewish tradition. Likewise, there is a parallel disunity within Jewry concerning Jewish observance. As far as Orthodoxy is concerned, it is in theory a system of law, going back consistently and without interruption for thousands of years to the beginning of Jewish history. All the elaborations of halakhah in the later Orthodox codes are held to be rediscoveries rather than novelties. Yet this picture of an eternal developing legal system breaks down when we face its astonishing shrinkages in contemporary society – great areas of Jewish law have disappeared for a wide variety of reasons. Frequently, individuals who consider themselves Orthodox have simply ceased to resort to rabbinical courts in numerous areas of life. There is thus a large gap between the Orthodox system of practice and the limited observance of Jewish life within a large segment of the Orthodox Jewish community.

The rapidly contracting area of observance within Orthodoxy is in part the reason for the existence of Conservative Judaism. Since its inception, Conservative rabbis have been anxious to make Jewish law more flexible so as to provide for change legally. This approach to the tradition has provided a framework for the reinterpretation of Jewish law in the light of changed circumstances and modern needs. While acknowledging the historical importance of the Jewish heritage, the movement has sought to discover new ways to adjust the legal system where necessary. As a result, many traditional observances have been abandoned and other features altered to suit contemporary circumstances. In this way Conservative Judaism has provided a means of legitimizing deviations from tradition, thereby contributing to the further shrinkage of the Jewish legal code.

Similarly, within Reform Judaism there has been an attempt to reinterpret Jewish law in the light of contemporary conditions. As the Reform Jewish scholar, Solomon Freehof, explained in *Reform Responsa*:

> Some of its provisions have passed from our lives. We do not regret that fact. But as to those laws that we do follow, we wish them to be in harmony with tradition ... Our concern is more with people than with the legal system. Wherever possible, such interpretations are developed which are feasible and conforming to the needs of life. Sometimes, indeed, a request must be answered in the negative when there is no way in the law for a permissive answer to be given. Generally the law is searched for such opinion as can conform with the realities of life.[12]

Due to such a liberal approach to tradition, even greater areas of the legal system have been rejected within the ranks of Reform Judaism. For many Reform Jews, traditional Jewish law has no bearing on their everyday lives.

Across the religious spectrum, then, there is wide divergence concerning Jewish observances and ceremonies. At the far right, traditional Orthodox Jews scrupulously adhere to the tradition, yet within the Orthodox camp there are many who have ignored the dictates of Jewish law. Within Conservative Judaism, deviation from the halakhah is legitimized, resulting in the abandonment of large areas of the tradition. And on the left, within Reform Judaism, there is a virtual abandonment of the traditional Code of Jewish Law. Beyond these major religious movements, many Reconstructionist and Humanistic Jews, as well as adherents of Jewish Renewal, have likewise abandoned the legal tradition. Similarly, modern kabbalists, Jewish feminists, Jewish ecologists, Gay and Lesbian Jews and others have selectively chosen those aspects of the tradition that they regard as spiritually significant.

Surveying such variations of practice, it is possible to isolate a number of criteria that have been loosely used to determine whether Orthodox laws should be retained. In some cases particular laws are retained simply because they have been followed for centuries. In other cases, an appeal is made to the spirit as opposed to the letter of the law. Alternatively, particular observances are adopted if they are grounded in biblical Judaism, even if they run counter to present-day Orthodoxy. On other occasions, traditional law is abandoned because it is not well adapted to modern life, or because it undermines the status of women. Unseemly rituals are also neglected, as are practices that appear to be based on superstition. Choices about Jewish practice are thus ultimately motivated by personal considerations, resulting in a lack of consistency and coherence. Hence, within Judaism today there is no agreement about either practice or religious belief: the unified character of traditional Judaism as it existed from ancient times to the Enlightenment has been replaced by chaos and confusion.

Jewish Peoplehood Under Threat

The fragmentation of Judaism into a variety of movements has brought about a major revolution in Jewish life today. No longer is it possible to speak of one people with a common heritage. Rather, as we have seen, the various segments of Jewry subscribe to radically different ideologies and religious orientations – in the history of the Jewish faith there has been no precedent for the coexistence of so many rival systems. Such a proliferation of interpretations of Judaism has given rise to a widespread concern about the nature of Jewish identity in the modern world. Pre-eminent among issues facing Jewry are the problems of intermarriage, divorce and conversion, which have brought about irresolvable fissures in the Jewish community.

According to Jewish law, if a Jewish woman is divorced she must obtain a valid religious bill of divorce (get) from her previous husband. Otherwise, any children of a subsequent marriage are deemed illegitimate (mamzerim) since they are considered to have been born adulterously (because the woman is viewed as still married to her former husband). In Jewish law such children are only allowed to marry other mamzerim or proselytes. As early as the 1840s, however, German reformers were beginning to abandon this religious procedure in favour of a civil divorce. Thus, the nineteenth-century reformer Samuel Holdheim argued that, as a result of emancipation, whatever has reference to inter-human relationships of a political, legal and civil character should no longer come under the province of biblical and rabbinic law. Rather, the rabbinic principle that 'the law of the land is the law' should apply to such cases. —ie. civil law not religious law

Such a rejection of halakhah has widespread implications, given the high incidence of divorce in contemporary society. In the past few decades the Jewish divorce rate in Western countries has increased enormously. By 1971, for example, the National Jewish Population Survey revealed that among the 25- to 29-year-old group, 15 per cent were separated or divorced. Such a statistic, combined with the fact that non-Orthodox groups constitute the majority of American Jews, led the Orthodox scholar Irving Greenberg to conclude that there would be approximately one to two hundred thousand mamzerim in America by the first decade of the twenty-first century. Even though such predictions have been challenged by other writers, there is no ① doubt that the growing number of mamzerim will be acute in the future, thereby deepening the schism between Orthodox and non-Orthodox Judaism.

② A second dilemma concerns conversion to Judaism. According to Jewish law, an individual is Jewish if he or she is born of a Jewish mother – otherwise a formal process of conversion is required. Such a procedure involves immersion in a mikveh (ritual bath), circumcision for males, and the acceptance of the divine commandments. Yet within the various branches of non-Orthodox Judaism, various features of the traditional process of conversion have been altered. In Reform Judaism, for example, immersion and circumcision are not universally required; there is no obligation to accept the Code of Jewish Law; the requirement that conversion procedures should take place in the presence of a rabbinic court of law is not invariably observed; and the traditional ruling that one must not convert for the sake of marriage has been ignored. As a result, all conversions undertaken outside the auspices of Orthodoxy have been rejected by the Orthodox establishment. This lack of recognition of non-Orthodox conversion has resulted in widespread confusion about Jewish identity. Today, a large number of those who are deemed Jewish by the various branches of non-Orthodox Judaism are regarded as Gentiles by the Orthodox.

Linked with this intractable difficulty about conversion has been the ruling by American Reform Judaism concerning Jewish descent. In 1983 the Reform movement decreed that a child is presumed to be Jewish if either of their parents is Jewish, as long as timely and appropriate acts of identification with the Jewish faith and people have taken place. By expanding the determination of Jewishness to include children of both matrilineal and patrilineal descent, the Reform movement thus defined as Jews individuals whom the other branches of Judaism regard as Gentiles. This means that neither these persons nor their descendants can be accepted as Jews by the non-Reform religious community.

Patrilineal Descent

On 15 March 1983 the Central Conference of American Rabbis (CCAR), the Reform movement's body of rabbis, passed a resolution prepared by a committee on patrilineal descent entitled: 'The Status of Children of Mixed Marriages':

Although the Hebrew Bible defines Jewish identity in patrilineal terms, the Mishnah states that the offspring of a Jewish mother and a non-Jewish father is recognized as a Jew, while the offspring of a non-Jewish mother and a Jewish father is considered a non-Jew. This Talmudic position became normative in Jewish law.

But the 1983 resolution was not the first attempt to reconsider patrilineality. Previously, many Reform rabbis quietly integrated the children of Jewish fathers and non-Jewish mothers into their religious schools and confirmed them into the Jewish faith along with their peer group in lieu of conversion. In 1947, the CCAR adopted a resolution that stated that if a Jewish father and a gentile mother wanted to raise their children as Jewish, 'the declaration of the parents to raise them as Jews shall be deemed sufficient for conversion' …

By 1983 the CCAR was ready to spell out the patrilineal descent resolution in greater detail. By this time there was a broad-based commitment to egalitarianism. To many, it seemed unnecessarily biased to accept the child of a Jewish mother and a gentile father as Jewish while rejecting the child of a Jewish father and a gentile mother. It seemed unfair that children of Jewish mothers who had no Jewish education were being given automatic recognition while children of Jewish fathers who received intense Jewish upbringings were not. Even more importantly, the rising intermarriage rate made it imperative that the net of Jewish identity be cast as widely as possible.[13]

The rift between Orthodoxy and the various denominations of non-Orthodox Judaism concerning personal status has important consequences for the State of Israel. From its inception, Israel has been determined to provide a homeland for Jewry; this principle is enshrined in the Law of Return. According to this law, any Jew who wishes to live in Israel can become a citizen without undergoing a naturalization procedure. As amended in 1970, the Law of Return states that a Jew is one born to a Jewish mother or who has been converted to Judaism. In subsequent years there have been innumerable attempts by the religious parties to amend the Law of Return so that only those who have been converted according to halakhah are deemed Jewish and thereby eligible to settle in the State of Israel. If accepted, such an alteration would render invalid all conversions undertaken by the Conservative or Reform rabbinate.

Law of Return

The Law of Return is Israeli legislation, enacted in 1950, that gives Jews, those of Jewish ancestry, and their spouses the right to migrate and settle in Israel and gain citizenship:

On 5 July 1950 the Knesset, Israel's Parliament, enacted the Law of Return. This law gives a legal basis for one of the objectives of the Zionist movement – to provide a solution to the Jewish people's problem by the re-establishment of a home for the Jewish people in Eretz Yisrael. In the Law of Return, the State of Israel put into practice the Zionist movement's credo as pledged in Israel's Declaration of Independence and recognized by the League of Nations in 1922, when charging Britain with the duty of establishing a Jewish National Home, and by the United Nations within the Partition Plan of 1947 which provided for the establishment of Israel as an independent Jewish state.[14]

Over the years Jewish thinkers have proposed a number of solutions to such challenges to Jewish peoplehood. For example, in 1956 the Orthodox halakhic authority, Moses Feinstein, delivered a ruling that aimed to dissolve the problem of the status of children of Reform second marriages. According to Feinstein, a marriage ceremony itself is invalid if it is not observed by two witnesses. Since those present at Reform marriages are most likely to be Reform Jews, it is probable that they transgress Jewish law in ways that disqualify them as witnesses. Thus Reform marriages are not halakhically valid, and therefore need no valid divorce. As a consequence, children from remarriages should not be considered mamzerim. Although previous authorities held that, regardless of the validity of the ceremony, the marriage was established by cohabitation, Feinstein maintained that this could not be so since this was not the intent of the couple, as everyone assumed that the marriage was established by the synagogue ceremony. By annulling all Reform marriages, Feinstein's aim was to remove the status of illegitimacy from the children of remarriages where the first marriage had been conducted under Reform auspices. Not surprisingly, however, many Reform rabbis were scandalized by this ruling. By rendering Reform marriages halakhically non-existent, Feinstein implicitly denied Reform's authenticity – thus, instead of healing rifts that divide modern Jewry, this proposal exacerbated the tensions that exist between the different movements.

Another solution to the fragmentation of Jewish peoplehood was proposed by the Chief Rabbi of the British Commonwealth, Jonathan Sacks, in *One People?* In his view, the divisions in the Jewish world must be overcome by an attitude of inclusivism that acknowledges that God's covenant is with all Jews. A philosophy of Jewish inclusivism, he believes, calls for a number of positive steps. First, inclusivists must be sensitive to the ways in which non-Orthodox Jews are described: 'We may not speak of other Jews except in the language of love and respect.' Further, inclusivists should not seek to use coercive means to bring these individuals back to tradition; rather they should seek to draw Jews to Torah-observant Judaism by words of 'peace' and 'cords of love'.

Within such an inclusivist perspective, education must be regarded as supremely important:

> The inclusivist recognizes that education must speak to the cultural situation. For it is through constant study that Torah is transformed from external law to internalized command ... The inclusivist recognizes that education must speak to the cultural situation of the student ... He knows that 'learning leads to doing', that education is Judaism's classic alternative to coercion, and that secular culture can only be confronted ... by an intensification of Jewish learning.[15]

Moreover, the inclusivist should seek to apply halakhah to its widest possible constituency. In this regard, he should aim to attain a nuanced understanding of other secular and liberal Jews. 'In so doing', Sacks argues, 'he relies on the general inclusivist argument that secular and liberal Jews are not to be judged as deliberate rebels but as unwitting or coerced products of their environment.' Even though Sacks cannot countenance the religious interpretation of non-Orthodox Judaism, he stresses that the various branches of non-Orthodoxy play a role in keeping alive the value of Jewish identity, faith and practice for many Jews. Regarding Israelis, Sacks insists that whatever their religious attitudes, they should be seen as fulfilling the command of 'settling in the land', which has traditionally been regarded by some scholars as equivalent to all the other commandments combined.

The inclusivist should also acknowledge that Jewish liberalism and secularism has given new life to some aspects of tradition. Secular Zionism, for example, has reminded Jews that political activity is part of Judaism; secularists and liberals have revived the Hebrew language, the Jewish national ideal, prophetic commitment to social action, and interest in rabbinic sources and medieval literature. Nonetheless, the inclusivist has the duty to call on liberal and secular Jewish leaders to act responsibly in the context of the totality of Judaism and the Jewish people. In particular, he should warn against the laxity of non-Orthodox conversions and the Reform ruling about patrilineal descent as well as its endorsements of homosexuality, premarital sex, and abortion on demand.

Here then, is a plea for all Jews – whether Orthodox or non-Orthodox – to recognize their common ancestry and shared peoplehood. From the Orthodox side, Sacks entreats his co-religionists to refrain from hurling abuse at those who have rejected halakhah. Such a stance of tolerance and understanding should help ameliorate the conflict between the various branches of contemporary Judaism, yet Sacks' recommendations do not provide a basis for the unity he seeks. No doubt most non-Orthodox Jews would simply view his position as patronizing and imperialistic. Members of the various movements outlined in Chapter 4 wish to be respected for their own interpretations of Judaism, but this is precisely what Sacks refuses to do.

Orthodoxy, Sacks maintains, is the true path and he is anxious to bring all Jews to recognition of this truth. Thus he wrote: 'The inclusivist faith is that Jews, divided by where they stand, are united by what they are travelling towards, the destination which alone gives meaning to Jewish history: the promised union of Torah, the Jewish people, the land of Israel, and God.'

For most Jews, however, there is no possibility of such a return. Inclusivist Orthodoxy thus fails to provide a unifying theology that can hold together the scattered fragments of the Jewish community.

Chapter 6

The Future of Judaism

Throughout this book, we have seen that Judaism has undergone fundamental changes since the time of the Enlightenment. No longer is Jewry united by a unified system of belief and practice. Instead, a wide variety of Jewish groupings has emerged, each with a different ideology and philosophy of Judaism. In addition, the events of the Holocaust and creation of the State of Israel have profoundly affected Jewish consciousness. Further, Jews today face a number of important social and ethical dilemmas. Given these changed circumstances, what is now required is an entirely new orientation to Jewish life if Judaism is to continue as a vibrant religious tradition. Arguably, such a reinterpretation of the Jewish heritage should be based on a revised vision of Judaism in which the traditional view of God's nature and activity is not seen as definitive and final. Rather, the Jewish faith should be perceived simply as one way among many of making sense of Divine Reality. Aware of the inevitable subjectivity of all religious belief, Jews should feel free to draw from the past those elements of the Jewish heritage that they regard as spiritually meaningful. Such a new philosophy of Judaism – distinct from the major religious Jewish movements that exist in the modern world – would acknowledge the true character of Jewish life today, and extol the principle of personal freedom that has become the hallmark of the modern age.

The Inadequacies of Contemporary Judaism

As we have observed, in the post-Enlightenment world Jewry is no longer unified by a cohesive religious system. Instead the Jewish people has fragmented into a wide range of subgroups espousing competing interpretations of the tradition. All of these movements seek to provide a basis for

Jewish existence in contemporary society, yet in different ways their solutions are inadequate and none is able to provide a universally acceptable philosophy for the community as a whole. Orthodox Judaism in its various forms, for example, has generally not faced up to the serious challenges posed to religion by science. Modern scientific discoveries have illustrated that the biblical account of creation is no longer credible and that traditional belief in the resurrection of the dead is implausible. Further, the scientific explanation of history has replaced the more primitive interpretation of biblical events. In addition, the critical findings of biblical scholars have illustrated that the doctrine of Torah MiSinai is fundamentally flawed. In the light of the findings of biblical archaeology and textual analysis it is inconceivable that Moses could have been the author of the Pentateuch. Orthodox thinkers have also failed to recognize the serious theological implications of the Holocaust. For many Jews the belief in an all-powerful and benevolent Deity who lovingly watches over his chosen people is no longer believable. Rather than providing a persuasive defence of theism, Orthodox leaders have simply affirmed the central tenets of the faith without seeking to demonstrate their validity.

Like Orthodox Judaism, Hasidism also has not come to terms with the findings of biblical scholarship. Unwilling to confront the overwhelming evidence that the Torah was composed at different times in the history of ancient Israel, Hasidic Jews proclaim – without providing a justification for their view – that God revealed the Torah in its entirety to Moses on Mount Sinai and that therefore the prescriptions contained in Scripture are authoritative. Moreover, Hasidic writers piously accept cosmological doctrines without acknowledging that these theories conflict with scientific investigations into the origin of the universe. The concept of the zaddik as a spiritually elevated individual able to act as an intermediary on behalf of his people is also unquestioningly accepted, even though most Jews have rejected such a notion of authoritarianism. A final difficulty with Hasidic theology concerns the concept of divine providence: to the modern mind it is inconceivable that human suffering, particularly during the Nazi period, could be the result of divine providence. For most Jews the religious ideas and lifestyle of Hasidism, as well as its perception of the role of women in society, are outmoded relics from a bygone age.

Traditional Judaism and Women

Within Orthodox and Hasidic Judaism, women are exempt from all positive, time-bound commandments and so have no obligation to take part in communal prayer and worship. The different morning blessings for men and women are instructive:

> **All say:** Blessed art thou, O Lord our God, King of the Universe, who has not made me a heathen.
> Blessed art thou, O Lord our God, King of the Universe, who has not made me a slave.
> **Men say:** Blessed art thou, O Lord our god, King of the Universe, who hast not made me a woman.
> **Women say:** Blessed art thou, O Lord our God, King of the Universe, who hast made me according to thy will.[1]

Moving across the religious spectrum, Reform Judaism is also beset with various difficulties, even though its supporters maintain that it provides a relevant form of Judaism for contemporary Jewry. The main difficulty with Reform is that it has failed to provide a coherent framework for belief and practice. With respect to religious convictions, sociological studies reveal that religious opinion within the movement ranges from traditional belief to atheism. And, as in the sphere of religious doctrine, there is a comparable disagreement with regard to Jewish law. Even though Reform Judaism has attempted to provide a common basis for Jewish practice, reformers have been unable to reach a consensus about which traditional laws should be retained: in attempting to formulate a modern Code of Jewish Law, subjective judgement prevails. As a consequence, modern Reform Judaism lacks a coherent ideology for its adherents.

In a similar vein Conservative Judaism suffers from a lack of coherence. Within the movement there is considerable uncertainty about the status of Jewish belief and practice. Some traditionalists, for example, assert that Scriptural and rabbinic law is authoritative for the Jewish people; others demand halakhic change. Regarding theological beliefs, some thinkers view God as a personal, supernatural being active in history; others contend that God should be conceived in non-personal terms since his nature transcends human understanding. At the other end of the spectrum, there are some Conservative writers who reject the notion of supernaturalism altogether. In their view God should be understood as a creative power in the cosmos. Similarly, disagreement also exists about the doctrine of revelation. Some more traditionally minded Conservative Jews believe that God revealed the Torah, even though not every word in the Pentateuch was communicated to Moses; other writers, however, interpret revelation as a process of divine encounter.

Another area of dispute concerns the belief that Jews are God's chosen people. Despite the fact that the Conservative prayer book has retained the traditional formula 'You have chosen us from all the nations', for many Conservative Jews the notion of chosenness must be modified to account for God's active involvement in the life of all human beings. Hence, like Reform Judaism, Conservatism is bedevilled with disagreement over the most central aspects of the tradition.

Reconstructionist Judaism differs from these other forms of Judaism in that it has explicitly rejected a belief in an external Deity. Under the influence of Mordecai Kaplan, Reconstructionist Jews have sought to reinterpret Judaism to meet the demands of modern life. In his writings, Kaplan argued that it is no longer possible to believe in a supernatural Deity; instead he maintained that the idea of God must be redefined. Promoting a naturalistic explanation of transcendence, Kaplan called for the re-establishment of a network of organic Jewish communities that would ensure the self-perpetuation of the Jewish heritage. The central difficulty with such a view is that, on the one hand, Reconstructionism has deliberately eliminated any form of theism from its philosophy, while, on the other, it has retained the central features of the Jewish faith. Thus, although Reconstructionist Jews do not believe in a God who responds to prayer, in practice their worship is essentially no different from what takes place in traditional synagogues. Similarly, the religious observances of Reconstructionist Judaism parallel what is found in Conservative Judaism but they are in no way connected with God's decree. Reconstructionism therefore is riddled with internal inconsistency: as a movement it seeks to perpetuate a traditional Jewish lifestyle while simultaneously rejecting the religious foundations on which such an adherence to the Jewish heritage has previously been based.

Like Reconstructionist Judaism, Jewish Humanism has also rejected a belief in a supernatural God. Yet – distancing itself from Reconstructionism – it has sought to provide an alternative lifestyle consonant with the principles of the movement. Extolling humane values, it strives to offer a mode of Jewish existence attuned to the modern age. Even though such an ideology may appeal to some Jews drawn to secular ideology, it is difficult to see how it could serve as a basis for Jewish living in contemporary society. In the light of the horrific events of the Holocaust, it has become increasingly difficult for most Jews to be confident about human progress. The basic assumptions of Humanistic Judaism are thus at odds with a growing sense of pessimism about the human potential for evil. Further, Humanist Judaism's reformulation of Jewish life-cycle events and holidays would in all likelihood hold little attraction for the vast majority of Jews, who are currently seeking for spiritual sustenance from the tradition.

It is clear, then, that none of these major movements – Orthodoxy, Hasidism, Reform Judaism, Conservative Judaism, Reconstructionist Judaism or Jewish Humanism – is adequate for the modern age. What is now required is a new interpretation of Judaism that acknowledges the depth of Jewish diversity and embraces the various and diverse forms of modern Judaism, including Jewish Buddhism, Jewish Renewal, Kabbalistic Judaism, Jewish Feminism and Jewish Vegetarianism and Ecology. The central feature of this new conception – which I will refer to as Pluralistic Judaism – is the principle of personal autonomy. Pluralistic Judaism would allow all individuals the right to select those features from the Jewish heritage that they find spiritually meaningful.

Unlike the major branches of modern Judaism, this new conception of the tradition would espouse a truly liberal doctrine of individual freedom, seeking to grant persons full religious independence. Adherents of Pluralistic Judaism would be actively encouraged to make up their own minds about religious belief and practice. It might be objected that such extreme liberalism would simply result in chaos – such criticism, however, fails to acknowledge the state of religious diversity already existent within Jewish society. Within the main branches of Judaism, there has been a gradual erosion of centralized authority; although many rabbis have attempted to establish standards for the members of their communities, there is a universal recognition that, in the end, all Jews will define for themselves which aspects of their heritage are personally relevant. In short, today there is a conscious acceptance of the principle of personal autonomy, even if in some quarters it is only grudgingly accepted. Pluralistic Judaism would hence be in accord with the spirit of the age. Its endorsement of personal decision-making would be consonant with the nature of modern Jewish existence. Grounded in an acceptance of the nature of the contemporary Jewish community, its philosophy reflects the realities of everyday life, in Israel and the diaspora.

A Theology of Pluralistic Judaism

As we observed in Chapter 1, for over two millennia Jews have maintained that the Torah was given by God to Moses on Mount Sinai. Such a belief served as the basis for the conviction that the Five Books of Moses – including history, theology and legal precepts – have absolute authority. As a result, Orthodox Judaism and Hasidism refuse to accept any modernist interpretations of the Pentateuch. Arguably, however, what is now required is a new theological understanding that will provide a framework for Jewish existence for the next millennium. What is needed is a theological structure consonant with a contemporary understanding of Divine Reality. In recent years an increasing number of theologians have called for a Copernican revolution in our understanding of religion. In their view, Divine Reality as it is in itself should be distinguished from Divine Reality as conceived in human thought and experience. Such a contrast, they point out, is in fact a major feature of many of the world's faiths.

As far as Judaism is concerned, throughout the history of the faith there has been a conscious awareness of such a distinction between God as He is in himself and human conceptions of the Divine. Scripture, for example, frequently cautions against describing God anthropomorphically. Thus the Book of Deuteronomy states: 'Therefore take good heed to yourselves. Since you saw no form on the day that the Lord spoke to you at Horeb out of the midst of the fire' (Deut. 4:5). Again, Exodus 33:20 declares:

> And he said, 'You cannot see my face; for man shall not see me, and live.' And the Lord said, 'Behold there is a place by me where you shall stand upon the rock; and while my glory passes I will put you in a cleft of the rock, and I will cover you with my hand until I have passed by; then I will take away my hand, and you shall see my back; but my face shall not be seen.'

In rabbinic literature there are comparable passages suggesting that human beings should refrain from attempting to describe God. Thus the Palestinian teacher Abin said: 'When Jacob of the village of Neboria was in Tyre, he interpreted the verse "For thee, silence is praise, O God" to mean that silence is the ultimate praise of God. It can be compared to a jewel without price: however high you appraise it, you will undervalue it.' In another talmudic passage a story is told of the man at prayer who was rebuked by the scholar Hanina. This individual praised God by listing as many of his attributes as he could. When he finished, Hanina asked if he had exhausted the praises of God. Hanina then said that even the three attributes 'The Great', 'The Valiant' and 'The Tremendous' could not legitimately be used to describe God were it not for the fact that Moses used them and they subsequently became part of the Jewish liturgy. This text concludes with a parable: if a king who possesses millions of gold pieces is praised for having millions of silver pieces such praise disparages his wealth rather than glorifies it.

The latter development of such a view was continued by both Jewish philosophers and mystics. In his treatise *Duties of the Heart*, for example, the eleventh-century philosopher Bahya Ibn Pakudah argued that the concept of God's unity involves the negation from God of all human and infinite limitations. According to Bahya, if we wish to ascertain the nature of anything, we must ask two fundamental questions: (1) if it is; and (2) what it is. Of God, however, it is possible to ask only if He is. And once having established his existence, it is not possible to go on to enquire about his nature, since it is beyond human comprehension. Arguing along similar lines, the twelfth-century Jewish philosopher Moses Maimonides focused on the concept of negative attributes. For Maimonides the ascription to God of positive attributes is a form of idolatry because it suggests that his attributes are coexistent with him. To say that God is one, Maimonides contended, is simply a way of negating all plurality from his being. Even when one asserts that God exists, one is simply affirming that his non-existence is impossible. Positive attributes are only admissible if they are understood as referring to God's acts. Attributes that refer to his nature, however, are only permissible if they are applied negatively. Moreover, the attributes that refer to God's actions imply only the acts themselves – they do not refer to the emotions from which these actions are generated when performed by human beings.

Following Maimonides, the fifteenth-century philosopher Joseph Albo in his *Ikkarim* maintained that God's attributes, referring to God's nature, can only be employed in a negative sense. On the other hand, attributes that refer to God's acts can be used positively as long as they do not imply change in God:

> But even the attributes in this class, those taken from God's acts, must be taken in the sense involving perfection, not in the sense involving defect. Thus, although these attributes cause emotion in us and make us change from one of the contraries to the other, they do not necessitate any change or emotions in God, for his ways are not our ways, nor are his thoughts our thoughts.

Like these Jewish philosophers, Jewish mystics advocated a theory of negation in describing God. For these kabbalists, the Divine is revealed through the powers that emanate from him. Yet God as he is in himself is the En Sof (Infinite). As the twelfth-century kabbalist Azriel of Gerona remarked: 'Know that the En Sof cannot be thought of, much less spoken of, even though there is a hint of it in all things, for there is nothing else apart from it. Consequently, it can be contained neither by letter nor name nor writing nor anything.' Similarly the *Zohar* (Book of Splendour) asserts that the En Sof is incomprehensible. It is only through the sefirot (divine emanations) that God is manifest in the world. Yet Jewish mystics were anxious to stress that the Divine is a unity. Hence a prayer in the *Zohar* ascribed to Elijah stresses the unity of the En Sof and the sefirot: 'Elijah began to praise God saying: Lord of the universe! You are one but are not numbered. You are higher than the highest. You are above all mysteries. No thought can grasp you at all.'

The Sefirot

The sefirot emanate successively from above to below, each one revealing a stage in the process. The common order of the sefirot are:

1. Crown (Keter)
2. Wisdom (Hokhmah)
3. Understanding (Binah)
4. Love (Hesed)
5. Strength (Gevurah)
6. Beauty (Tiferet)
7. Victory (Netzah)
8. Splendour (Hod)
9. Foundation (Yesod)
10. Kingship (Malkhut)[2]

According to the *Zohar* even the higher realms of the Divine – the stages represented by God's will, wisdom and understanding (Keter, Hokhmah and Binah) – should be understood negatively. Thus, God's will, which is represented by the sefirah Keter, is referred to as Ayin (Nothingness) – it is so elevated beyond human understanding that it can only be represented by negation. Concerning divine wisdom, represented by Hokhmah, the *Zohar* declares that one can ask what it is but should expect no answer. Likewise the eighteenth-century scholar the Vilna Gaon stated that one can say so little about the En Sof that one should not even give it the name En Sof.

The En Sof

The *Zohar* asserts that the En Sof is incomprehensible. It is only through the sefirot (divine emanations) that the Divine is manifest in the World. Yet, Jewish mystics were anxious to stress that the Divine is a unity. Hence a prayer in the *Zohar* ascribed to Elijah stresses the unity of the En Sof and the sefirot (divine emanations):

Elijah began to praise God saying: Lord of the universe! You are one but are not numbered. You are higher than the highest. You are above all mysteries. No thought can grasp you at all. It is you who produced the ten perfections which we call the ten sefirot. With them you guide the secret worlds which have not been revealed and the worlds which have been revealed, and in them you conceal yourself from human beings. But it is you who binds them together and unites them. Since you are in them, whoever separates any one of these ten from the others it is as if he had made a division in you.[3]

Here then is a new theological framework – deeply rooted in the rabbinic, philosophical and mystical tradition – which can serve as a basis for a new vision of Jewish theology today. Acknowledging the limitation of human comprehension, such a way of unknowing reveals that there is no means by which to ascertain the true nature of Divine Reality as it is in itself. In the end, the doctrines of Judaism must be regarded as human images constructed from within particular social and cultural contexts. Thus the absolute claims about God as found in biblical and rabbinic literature which were surveyed in the first chapter should be understood as human conceptions stemming from the religious experience of the Jewish nation. Jewish monotheism – embracing myriad formulations from biblical through medieval to modern times – is grounded in the life of the Jewish people. In all cases, pious believers and thinkers expressed their understanding of God's activity on the basis of their own personal as well as communal encounter. Yet, given that Divine Reality as it is in itself is beyond human comprehension, this Jewish understanding of the Godhead cannot be viewed as definitive and final. Rather, it should be seen as only one among many ways in which human beings have attempted to make sense of the Ultimate. In this light it makes no sense for any of the various Jewish movements to believe that they possess the unique truth about God and his actions in the world. On the contrary, universalistic truth-claims about the Divine should give way to a recognition of the inevitable subjectivity of religious convictions.

The implications of this shift away from the absolutist of the Jewish past to a new vision of Jewish theology are radical and far-reaching. Judaism – like all other religions – has advanced absolute, universal claims about the nature of God, but, given the separation between our finite understanding and Ultimate Reality, there is no way of attaining complete certitude about the veracity of these beliefs. Divine Reality as it is in itself transcends human comprehension, and hence it must be admitted that Jewish religious convictions are no different in principle from those found in other religious traditions. All are lenses through which the Ultimate is conceptualized. The Jewish faith, like all other major religions, is built around its distinctive way of thinking and experiencing the Divine. Yet in the end Jews across the religious spectrum must remain agnostic about the correctness of their religious beliefs.

Reformulating Jewish Identity

According to Jewish law, a person born of a Jewish mother is regarded as Jewish. Conversely, however, an individual born of a Jewish father and a non-Jewish mother is not Jewish. Such a person is a Gentile. For thousands of years this has been the normative understanding of Jewish identification. This means that someone who is atheistic, agnostic or non-practising but born of a Jewish mother is nevertheless Jewish. Correct belief or observance is irrelevant. As a result of this legal definition of Jewish identity, there are many individuals today who, though formally recognized as Jews, are in no sense religious. Some of these individuals adamantly identify with the community; others refuse such identification. Yet, whatever their response, the Jewish community regards them as belonging to the Jewish fold and accords them various religious rights (such as the right to be married in a synagogue or buried in a Jewish cemetery). Here, then is a simple criterion of Jewishness.

In modern times, however, such a definition has been obscured for several reasons. First, the Gentile world has not invariably applied this legal criterion of Jewishness to the Jewish populace. Frequently – as took place in Nazi Germany – persons are considered Jews even if they do not qualify according to this internal Jewish classification. During the Third Reich, for example, the Citizen Laws defined persons as Jewish if they were simply of Jewish blood. This means that some of those murdered by the Nazis would not have been accepted as Jews by the Jewish community.

A second difficulty concerns the decision taken in 1983 by the Central Conference of American Rabbis (the body of American Reform rabbis) that a child of either a Jewish father or a Jewish mother should be deemed as Jewish, assuming that this presumption is confirmed by timely and appropriate acts of identification with the Jewish faith and people. By expanding the criterion of Jewishness to include children of both matrilineal and patrilineal descent the Reform movement thus defined as Jews individuals whom other branches of Judaism regard as Gentiles. Neither these persons nor their descendants are accepted as Jews by the Orthodox religious establishment.

A further difficulty about Jewish status concerns the process of conversion. According to tradition, a non-Jew is permitted to join the Jewish community by undergoing conversion. Orthodox Judaism specifies that conversion is a ritual process involving immersion in a ritual bath (mikveh) and circumcision for males. Conversion is to take place in the presence of a court of law (bet din). The procedure has remained constant through the ages; however, within the non-Orthodox branches of Judaism, there have been various modifications to this process. Conservative Judaism, for example, generally adopts the traditional procedure, but it does not always follow the precise legal requirements. For this reason, most Orthodox rabbis do not recognize Conservative conversions as valid. Similarly, since Reform Judaism has largely abandoned ritual immersion and does not conduct circumcision in the required form, its converts are not accepted by the Orthodox community. Thus, Reform and Conservative converts and their offspring as well as converts in the other non-Orthodox branches of Judaism are deemed to be Gentiles by the Orthodox establishment, and in consequence there is considerable confusion in the Jewish world as to who should be regarded as legitimately Jewish.

Reform Conversion

At a Reform conversion, the rabbi normally delivers a brief charge to the convert, and then asks the following questions:

1. Do you of your own free will seek admittance into the Jewish faith?
2. Have you given up your former faith and severed all other religious affiliations?
3. Do you pledge your loyalty to Judaism and to the Jewish people amid all circumstances and conditions?

4. Do you promise to establish a Jewish home and to participate actively in the life of the Synagogue and the Jewish community?
5. If you should be blessed with children, do you promise to rear them in the Jewish faith?

Is there any solution to this profound dilemma concerning Jewish status? Given the shift in orientation from the absolutism of the past, Pluralistic Judaism would be able to offer a new definition of Jewishness for the modern age. According to this new philosophy of Judaism, Jews should not regard the doctrines of their faith as the true expression of God's will. Rather, contemporary Jewry should adopt a more open stance in which God as He is in himself – instead of the Jewish conception of the Divine – is placed at the centre of the Universe of faiths. Such a stance would enable Jews to affirm the uniqueness of their own heritage while acknowledging the validity of other approaches to the Divine. As we have seen, the theology underpinning this shift of perspective is based on the distinction between God as He is in himself and Divine Reality as perceived. From this vantage point the truth-claims of all religious systems should be seen as human constructions rather than universally valid doctrines. As a consequence, the various interpretations of the Jewish faith should no longer be perceived as embodying God's final and decisive revelation for humanity.

Such a new vision of the Jewish heritage calls for a re-evaluation of the traditional commitment to belief and practice. In the past, Jewish doctrines were regarded as binding upon all Jews. No longer, however, is it possible to regard Judaism in this way. This new philosophy, in which the Jewish faith is regarded simply as one faith among many, calls for an attitude of openness. If the Jewish faith is ultimately a human construct growing out of the experience of the nation over four millennia, it must be susceptible to reinterpretation and change. Aware of the inevitable subjectivity of religious belief, all Jews should feel free to draw from the tradition those features that they find religiously significant. In other words, the authoritarianism of the past should give way to personal autonomy in which all persons are at liberty to construct for themselves a personal system of religious observance relevant to their own needs.

Such theological liberalism offers a new orientation to the current perplexities regarding Jewish identity. A solution to the problem is to redefine Jewishness – with Pluralistic Judaism's non-dogmatic reinterpretation of religious doctrine, there is no reason to regard the traditional legal understanding of Jewishness as binding. Instead Jewish identity could be redefined along the lines suggested by Humanistic Judaism. Humanistic Jews are anxious to avoid any form of racism in their definition of Jewishness; similarly, they do not seek to impose a religious test on converts. Rather, they desire to accept within the Jewish fold all those who wish to identify themselves with the Jewish people.

Similarly, Pluralistic Judaism – with its emphasis on religious openness and personal autonomy – could offer a similar definition of Jewishness. Distancing itself from either biological descent or correct belief and practice, Pluralistic Judaism would welcome as Jews all those, regardless of ancestry, who desire to be identified in this fashion. On this basis, Jewish identity would be solely a matter of personal choice. In other words, Jewishness would be construed as an optional identification rather than the result of matrilineal or patrilineal descent or religious conversion formally accepted by a rabbinic body. Being a Jew would then be an option open to all. Although such reinterpretation of Jewish status would not be acceptable to the major branches of Judaism, it would eliminate the uncertainty surrounding the question: who is a Jew? Pluralistic Judaism's simple answer would be: all those who wish to adopt such an identification.

A related complication about Jewish status, which could be resolved by the principles of this new philosophy of Judaism, concerns the remarriage of female Jews who, though divorced in civil law, have failed to obtain a Jewish bill of divorce (get). As mentioned earlier, Orthodox Judaism does not recognize their divorces as valid, and any subsequent liaison, even when accompanied by a non-Orthodox Jewish marriage ceremony or civil marriage, is regarded as adulterous. Further, the children of such unions are stigmatized as illegitimate (mamzerim) and barred from marrying other Jews unless they are also mamzerim or proselytes. Reform Judaism – as well as other non-Orthodox movements – has abandoned this religious procedure in favour of civil divorce; a rejection of Jewish law that has widespread implications. Given the high incidence of divorce in contemporary society, there are a considerable number of mamzerim in the Jewish community today, thereby deepening the schism between Orthodox and non-Orthodox Jewry.

The traditional procedure for divorce is based on the Code of Jewish Law:

> The officiating rabbi initially asks the husband if he gives the bill of divorce (get) of his own free will and without duress and compulsion. After receiving the writing materials from a scribe, he instructs the scribe to write a get. The get is then read and the rabbi again asks

the husband if the get is given freely. The wife is then asked if she freely accepts the get. The rabbi tells the wife to remove all jewellery from her hands and hold her hands out, with open palms upward, to receive the bill of divorce. The rabbi then gives the get to her husband; he holds it in both hands and drops it into the palms of the wife and states: 'This be your get and with it be you divorced from this time forth so that you may become the wife of any man.'[4]

Pluralistic Judaism offers a simple solution to this problem. As we have seen, this new philosophy of Judaism would promote individual decision-making, unfettered by the religious restraints of the past. Extolling the principle of self-determination, Pluralistic Judaism would encourage all persons to exercise their personal autonomy in determining which aspects of the tradition they wish to retain or discard. Departing from the legalism of the past as well as from the prescriptive nature of the various branches of non-Orthodoxy, Pluralistic Judaism would therefore provide a basis for the wholesale rejection of the category of mamzer: this would mean that the children of all remarriages undertaken without first obtaining a get would be regarded as untainted by the stigma of illegitimacy. Such a solution has, of course, already been advocated by the Reform community itself – the status of being a mamzer is deemed null and void. Nonetheless, the philosophy of Pluralistic Judaism provides an ideological basis for such a rejection: given Pluralistic Judaism's reinterpretation of religious doctrine, there is no reason to regard any traditional categories of Jewish status as binding on contemporary Jewry as a whole.

Jewish Belief in a New Age

As we observed in Chapter 1, in the past traditional Jews regarded the tenets of Judaism as absolute and final. For this reason the twelfth-century Jewish philosopher Moses Maimonides asserted that anyone who denies the cardinal principles of Judaism is a heretic. While less extreme than Orthodoxy, the various branches of non-Orthodox Judaism similarly have uncompromising views of religious belief. Reform, Conservative, Reconstructionist and Humanistic Jews, for example, contend that their respective worldviews are correct. Thus, across the Jewish spectrum, the varied theistic interpretations of the nature and activity of God as well as the perspectives of non-theistic Judaism are viewed as objectively valid.

Pluralistic Judaism, however, challenges such dogmatism. On the basis of the distinction between God as He is in himself and God as perceived, it is no longer credible to assert that one's religious views are categorically true. Within this framework of Pluralistic Judaism, various philosophies of the Jewish tradition as found in the various Jewish movements should be viewed as lenses through which Ultimate Reality has been differently conceptualized. The implications of this new outlook are of profound importance in the shaping of Judaism for the future. A philosophy of Judaism in which religious doctrines are seen as ultimately human in origin calls for an attitude of openness. Aware of the inevitable subjectivity of religious belief, absolute claims about God should be construed as human conceptions stemming from the experience of the Jewish people throughout their long history.

Religion as 'Experiencing-as'

According to the theologian John Hick, religious convictions should be understood as inevitably based on interpretation. In *Philosophy of Religion*, he argues that religious belief should be conceived as a form of 'experiencing-as':

> In our everyday perception of our environment, we use several sense organs at once: 'experiencing as' is an interpretive mode of cognition which operates even in commonplace situations. If, for example, a stone-age savage were shown knives and forks, he would not experience them as such because of his lack of the concept of eating at a table with manufactured implements. As far as religious belief is concerned, religious experience should be seen in similar terms. Throughout history human beings have displayed a tendency to experience individuals, places and situations as having religious meanings. It is clear that the way in which believers see the world depends on the system of concepts used. Such a view helps to explain why it is that the same features can be experienced in radically different ways.[5]

On the basis of this revised understanding of Jewish doctrine, Jewish monotheism – embracing myriad formulations from biblical through medieval to modern times – should be perceived as grounded in the life of the nation. In all cases, devout believers, thinkers and mystics have expressed their understanding of God's nature and activity on the basis of their own spiritual apprehension. Yet, given that God as He is in himself is beyond human comprehension, such a formulation should be viewed as only one mode among many different ways of apprehending the Divine. In this light, it makes no sense for Jews of whatever persuasion to believe that they possess unique truth about Ultimate Reality. On the contrary, universalistic truth-claims should give way to a recognition of the inevitable subjectivity of all convictions about God.

The same conclusion applies to Jewish beliefs about God's revelation. Instead of declaring that God uniquely disclosed his word to the Jewish people in the Hebrew Scriptures as well as through the teachings of rabbinic scholars, Jews should recognize that their Holy Writ is simply one record among many others. Both the Written and the Oral Torah have particular significance for Jewry, but this does not imply that these writings contain a uniquely true and superior divine disclosure. Instead, the Torah as well as rabbinic literature should be conceived as a record of the spiritual life of the nation and testimony of its religious quest. As such, it should be viewed in much the same light as the New Testament, the Qur'an, the Bhagavad-Gita, and the Vedas. For the Jewish people their own sacred literature has special significance, but it should not be regarded as possessing truth for all humankind.

Likewise the doctrine of the chosen people should be revised. In the past, Jews believed that God had chosen them from all peoples to be the bearer of his message. Although Jews have derived great strength from the conviction that God has a special relationship with Israel, such a belief is based on a misapprehension of Judaism in the context of the religious experience of humankind. Given that God as He is in himself transcends human understanding, the belief that God selected a specific people as his agent is nothing more than an expression of the Jewish people's sense of spiritual superiority and their impulse to disseminate its religious message. In fact, however, there is simply no way of determining if a single group stands in a unique relationship with God. Again, the ideology of Pluralistic Judaism challenges the traditional conviction that God has a providential plan for the Jewish people and for all humanity. The belief that God's guiding hand is manifest in all things is ultimately a human response to the universe. It is not, as Jews have believed through the centuries, certain knowledge. This is well illustrated by the fact that other traditions have proposed a similar view of both general and special providence, yet maintain that God's action in the world has taken an entirely different course. In other cases, non-theistic religions such as Buddhism have formulated conceptions of human destiny divorced from the activity of God or the gods. Such differences in interpretation highlight the subjective nature of all belief systems.

The Jewish conception of the Messiah should also be understood in a similar light. Within the scheme of Pluralistic Judaism, the longing for messianic deliverance should be perceived as a pious hope based on both personal and communal expectations. Although this conviction has served as a bed rock of the Jewish faith since biblical times, it is inevitably shaped by human conceptualization. Thus, like other doctrines in the Jewish tradition, it is grounded in the experience of the Jewish nation and has undergone a variety of reformulations in the course of the history of the nation. But because God as He is in himself is beyond human comprehension, there is simply no way of ascertaining whether the belief in a personal Messiah has foundation in fact.

Again, this new philosophical understanding of Judaism demands a similar stance concerning the doctrine of the afterlife. Although the belief in the eschatological unfolding of history has been a central feature of the Jewish heritage from rabbinic times to the present, it is simply impossible to determine whether these events will in fact occur in the future. In our finite world – limited by space and time – certain knowledge about such issues is unobtainable. Belief in an afterlife in which the righteous of Israel will receive their just reward has sustained the Jewish people through suffering, persecution and tragedy, yet from a pluralistic outlook these doctrines can be no more certain than any other elements of the Jewish religious tradition.

The implications of this shift from the absolutism of the past to a new vision of Jewish theology are radical and far-reaching. The various branches of modern Judaism including non-theistic movements have advanced absolute, universal truth claims about the nature of the universe – but given the separation between our finite understanding and God as He is in himself, there can be no way of attaining complete certainty about the veracity of these beliefs. God transcends human understanding, and hence it must be admitted that Jewish religious beliefs are in principle no different from those found in other religious faiths: all are lenses through which Ultimate Reality is conceptualized. Judaism, in its various forms, like all the other world religions, is built around its distinctive way of thinking and experiencing the Divine.

Given such an agnostic interpretation of the Jewish heritage, what belief system is appropriate for adherents of Pluralistic Judaism? For those who subscribe to this new philosophy of Judaism, there is a broad range of options. For those of a traditional disposition, it would be possible to adopt a mode of Judaism embracing the central features of the Jewish tradition. Here, an advocate of Pluralistic Judaism would accept the conventional picture of God as a supernatural Deity who created and sustains the universe. In essence, such a view would be the same as that found in Orthodox Judaism and Hasidism as well as in Conservative Judaism and the Reform movement. Yet there is one fundamental difference between conventional theism and theism as understood within this new philosophy of Judaism. For the traditionalist, this view of the Godhead is accepted unquestioningly – there is no debate about its validity. For followers of Pluralistic Judaism, on the other hand, religious belief would be conceived as a tentative hypothesis. Aware of the conjectural nature of all religious beliefs, Pluralists would acknowledge that their conceptualization of God is a humanly constructed concept by which God is understood.

Other adherents of Pluralistic Judaism might, however, desire to espouse a modified form of theism in which various elements of the traditional understanding of God are revised. Within Pluralistic Judaism such theological adjustments would be in harmony with its emphasis on personal decision-making. A cardinal aspect of this new Jewish ideology is the appropriateness of religious modification to the time-honoured doctrines of the faith. This signifies that all divine attributes as well as theological concepts could be subjected to change. Hence, the various modifications to traditional Orthodox teaching proposed by Reform, Conservative, Reconstructionist and Humanistic thinkers as well as adherents of Jewish Renewal, Kabbalistic Judaism, Jewish Feminism, Jewish Ecology, and so forth would be admissible. Moreover, there would be no compulsion for such altered notions to be accepted by all members of the community; on the contrary, it would be impossible for adherents of Pluralistic Judaism to formulate binding statements of belief. Instead, all persons would be encouraged to formulate their own personal interpretations of Judaism in accordance with their religious leanings.

Reinterpreting Jewish Practice

As we have seen in Chapter 2, until the time of the Enlightenment the Jewish people were united by a common religious inheritance. In the post-Enlightenment world, however, the Jewish community has broken up into a variety of subgroups espousing differing and competing ideologies. Thus, across the religious spectrum, there is a wide variety of interpretations of the tradition: Orthodox and Hasidic Judaism are dedicated to the perpetuation of biblical law as interpreted through the centuries by rabbinic sages. Conservative and Reconstructionist Judaism seek to preserve many of the central features of traditional Judaism while allowing for modifi-

cation. Reform and Humanistic Judaism actively encourage the reformulation of the Jewish tradition to meet contemporary circumstances. Beyond
these major movements, there is a wide range of subgroups, as surveyed
in Chapter 4, which variously interpret the Jewish heritage.

Alongside these differing movements, there is a broad range of observance among the adherents of each branch of Judaism. In each movement
there has been a gradual erosion of centralized authority. Although many
rabbis have attempted to establish standards for the members of their
communities, there is a universal recognition today that in the end all Jews
– regardless of formal affiliation – will define for themselves which aspects
of the Jewish tradition are personally relevant. Modern Jews are ultimately
guided by their own consciences. Moreover, the rabbinic establishment is
no longer able to impose sanctions on those who have ignored its rulings.
In short, in today's Jewish world there is a conscious acceptance of the
principle of personal autonomy even if in some quarters it is only reluc-
tantly accepted.

Conservative Judaism and the Torah

According to the Conservative scholar Ben Zion Bokser, modern
Jews must adapt the tradition to contemporary demands. Writing in
Jewish Law: A Conservative Approach, he states:

> Conservatism admits the propriety of change. It admits the
> divine origin of the Torah; but it asserts that, as we encounter it,
> every divine element is encumbered with a human admixture,
> that the divine element ... rests in specific forms which are
> historically conditioned. These historically conditioned forms
> are subject to adjustment.[6]

As an alternative to the more structured models of the Jewish faith represented by the various contemporary Jewish movements, Pluralistic Judaism
would provide a new foundation for dealing with the realities of modern
Jewish life. By advocating the principle of personal autonomy, its philosophy
would be in accord with the spirit of the age; its endorsement of individual
decision-making would be consonant with the nature of modern Jewish life.
Pluralistic Judaism is grounded in an acceptance of the nature of contemporary Jewish existence; its advocacy of individual liberty and freedom of
choice reflects the actual conditions of Jewish living in the twenty-first

century. The central feature of modern Jewish existence is the principle of personal autonomy despite a general lack of conscious recognition in the Jewish community of its pervasiveness. Pluralistic Judaism, however, not only acknowledges this characteristic of Jewish life; it celebrates freedom of choice as a positive virtue. In all spheres of activity, modern democratic societies foster individual decision-making; so, too, in the religious domain, should personal liberty – unrestrained by centralized coercion – be regarded as a cardinal axiom of any theological system. Unique among the various interpretations of Judaism, Pluralistic Judaism would endorse such a canon of action as its guiding rule.

As we have seen, the various branches of non-Orthodox Judaism do not accept biblical and rabbinic law as binding; in their different ways these movements have redefined the scope of Jewish law. Yet, despite such liberalism, all these movements are prescriptive in their interpretation of the legal tradition. Pluralistic Judaism, however, would stimulate all Jews to determine for themselves which Jewish practices should be followed. Thus, more traditionally minded supporters of Pluralistic Judaism might desire to follow the Orthodox pattern of Jewish observance, including daily worship, attendance at Sabbath and Festival services, and a strict adherence to ritual law. In terms of outward appearances, their Jewish lifestyle would resemble that of pious Orthodox, Conservative or Reconstructionist Jews. Indeed, such individuals might feel most comfortable as members of Orthodox, Conservative or Reconstructionist synagogues. Yet, as followers of this new philosophy of Judaism, they would acknowledge that their personal religious choices are no more valid than those of the less observant.

Jews less conservative in approach, on the other hand, might wish to abandon or modify various features of Jewish law. Such individuals, for example, might wish to distance themselves from the vast number of prescriptions surrounding Jewish worship, home observance and personal piety – instead they would seek to formulate a Jewish lifestyle more in keeping with the demands of modern life. As we have seen, this has been the policy of Reform Judaism from its inception. For these less observant Jews, Reform Judaism would in all likelihood offer the most adaptable religious stance. Nonetheless, even if they were members of a Reform congregation, as followers of Pluralistic Judaism they would acknowledge that their individual decisions should in no way set a standard for others. Rather, as exponents of this new liberated philosophy of Judaism, they would be under an obligation to respect the choices of all Jews, no matter how observant or lax.

Pluralistic Judaism would also accept as valid the resolve of Jews who desire to express only minimal recognition of their Jewishness. Such persons, for example, might choose to ignore Jewish law altogether in their everyday lives and only attend synagogue on the High Holy Days or for the yartzeit of a parent. Alternatively, they might simply wish to be married or buried under Jewish auspices without belonging to a synagogue. Pluralistic Judaism – as an all-embracing fluid system extolling personal autonomy as a fundamental tenet – would accept the legitimacy of even such a nominal form of Jewish identification.

This notion of Judaism as an amorphous religious system can perhaps best be illustrated by the analogy of the supermarket. If we imagine the past arranged in long aisles, and individual Jews with shopping trolleys, Pluralistic Judaism would encourage each person to select from the shelves those items he or she wishes to possess. Thus, for example, Orthodox and Hasidic Jews would leave with overflowing trolleys; Conservative, Reform and Reconstructionist Jews would depart with less, as would adherents of Jewish Renewal and modern Kabbalists; Humanistic Jews would leave with even fewer commodities; and non-affiliated Jews such as non-observant Israelis would depart with hardly any. This image of the supermarket emphasizes the non-judgemental character of Pluralistic Judaism. Just as when shopping, each person is able to make selections without fear of coercion or criticism, so within this open model of Judaism individuals would be able to decide for themselves which features of the Jewish past they desire to incorporate into their own lives. Shoppers in such a Jewish marketplace would be free agents, charting their own personal path through the tradition. Further, as in a supermarket where there is no critical assessment made by other shoppers or by the supermarket staff of the choices made, so within Pluralistic Judaism censorious evaluations of the decisions of others would have no place.

This philosophy of Judaism, as a new orientation to Judaism more in accord with the realities of everyday Jewish life, would welcome into the Jewish marketplace all those who seek such identification, regardless of their background. Pluralistic Judaism would regard all persons as members of the Jewish community if they wished to be included. In the past, Orthodoxy defined as Jews all those who are of maternal descent; in addition, traditional Judaism provided a formalized means of conversion, and recently Reform Judaism has modified this definition of Jewishness to include all those born of a Jewish mother or father. As we have seen, this has resulted in widespread uncertainty within the Jewish community as to who qualifies as a Jew. Pluralistic Judaism provides a simple solution to this dilemma: all those who desire to be known as Jews would be granted this status. The only criterion of Jewishness would be a sincere desire to identify in this way: all would be welcome in the Jewish marketplace and would be encouraged to chart their own way through the tradition without fear of coercion or criticism.

Pluralistic Judaism, therefore, as a philosophy of Judaism, does not set out to establish itself as an organized movement within the ranks of modern Jewry. Different from the various branches of religious Jewish life, with their own seminaries, rabbis, congregational structures and educational facilities, Pluralistic Judaism should be seen as a new ideology, a vision of Judaism based on a revised conception of the nature of God. Liberal in orientation, it offers all Jews – no matter what their particular religious affiliation – a remodelled conceptualization of Jewish life more in accordance with the realities of Jewish existence. As an overarching framework for Jewish observance, it respects the manifold religious choices made by Jews today. Within this framework, Jewish practice – whatever its form – is accepted as valid.

As a radical alternative to the more structured models of the Jewish faith, this new philosophy of Judaism provides a non-dogmatic foundation for integrating Jewish belief and practice into modern life. Such a fluid system, attuned to the realities of everyday life, provides a comprehensive vision of Jewish existence for the future. Unlike the current subgroups within the Jewish world, Pluralistic Judaism celebrates the plurality of Jewish belief and practice in the modern age. Respectful of the differences in the community, this new conception of Judaism – based on a recognition of the inevitable subjectivity of religious belief – furnishes an overarching ideological basis for Jewish living in a pluralistic age. As a remedy for the bitter divisions that beset the Jewish community, this new approach to the Jewish heritage offers the hope of unity beyond diversity for the next millennium.

The Future of Judaism and Global Theology

Given the shift away from the absolutism of the past, Pluralistic Judaism provides a radically new basis for interfaith encounter as well. Previously, Jewish thinkers argued that Judaism contains God's fullest revelation to humankind. Thus it is the superior religion, surpassing all rivals. Even the most liberal thinkers maintained that all human beings will eventually acknowledge the truth of Jewish monotheism. Such a belief is enshrined in the Amidah prayer recited in the Orthodox as well as non-Orthodox worship services:

Therefore do we hope in thee, O Eternal, our God! speedily to behold the effulgence of thy might, removing all idols, and utterly destroying man's vain creations; righting the world by Almighty sovereignty, so that all the children of flesh shall invoke thy name, and toward thee turn all the wicked of the earth. Then shall all the indwellers of the world recognise and clearly see, that unto thee all knees must bend, all tongues swear. In thy presence, O Eternal, Our God! shall they kneel and prostrate, ascribing honour to the glory of thy name, and taking upon themselves the yoke of thy supremacy, that thou mayest reign over them fully and for evermore. For sovereignty is thine, and for ever shalt thou reign in glory, as it is written in thy Law: The Eternal shall reign for ever and ever. And it is further said: The Eternal shall be King throughout the earth; on that day the Eternal shall be one, and his name one.

Today, however, in our religiously plural world, it is no longer possible to sustain such an exclusivist position – what is required instead is a redefinition of the theological exploration in view of the recognition that religious doctrines in all the world's faiths are simply human attempts to understand the nature of the Divine.

The pursuit of religious truth in a global context calls for a dialogical approach. The formation of a Jewish global, interreligious theology rests on two conditions. First, Jewish thinkers must endeavour to learn from traditions other than their own. Global theology undertaken from within the context of Pluralistic Judaism requires religious thinkers to investigate what the world's faiths have experienced and affirmed about the nature of Divine Reality, the phenomenon of religious experience, the nature of the self, the problem of the human condition, and the value of the world. Second, Jewish thinkers should endeavour to enter into the thought-world as well as religious experience of those of other faiths. This can only be achieved by being a participant in their way of life.

Global Theology

In our pluralistic world, modern theologians have stressed the importance of engaging with adherents of other religions. As Wilfred Cantwell Smith remarked:

> The time will soon be with us when a theologian who attempts to work out his position unaware that he does so as a member

of a world society in which other theologians equally intelligent, equally devout, equally oral, are Hindus, Buddhists, Muslims and unaware that his readers are likely perhaps to be Buddhists or to have Muslim husbands or Hindu colleagues – such a theologian is as out of date as is one who attempts to construct an intellectual position unaware that Aristotle has thought about the world or that existentialists have raised new orientations, or unaware that the earth is a minor planet in a galaxy that is vast only by terrestrial standards.[7]

Jewish thinkers must therefore strive to enter into the subjectivity of other religions and bring the resulting insights to bear on their own understanding of religion. Such reflection demands a multifaceted approach in which all religions are viewed as interdependent. With such a global perspective, those who embrace this new philosophy of Judaism should insist that this theological endeavour takes place in a transreligious context. This enterprise requires an encounter in which Jews confront others who hold totally dissimilar truth-claims; such individuals can help Jewish thinkers to discover their own underlying assumptions. In this process Jewish partners should be able to acknowledge the limitations of their own heritage, and as a result make a conscious effort to discover common ground with other faiths. Such interchange is vital to the foundation of a multidimensional religious outlook.

Not only would this new philosophy of Judaism provide a basis for a dialogical engagement with other faiths, it could provide a framework for engagement on a more practical level. No longer should Jews feel constrained to stand apart from the worship services of other religious traditions. Rather, a pluralist standpoint in which all faiths are recognized as authentic paths to Divine Reality would encourage the adherents of all faiths – including Jews – to engage in common religious activity. In this regard, a distinction should be made between three types of interfaith worship:

1. *Services of a particular religious community in which members of other faiths are invited as guests.* On such occasions, it is usual to ask a representative of the visiting faith-community to recite a suitable prayer or preach a sermon, but the liturgy remains the same.
2. *Interfaith gatherings of a serial nature.* At such meetings representatives of each religion offer prayers or readings on a common theme. Those present constitute an audience listening to a liturgical

anthology in which the distinctiveness of each religion is acknowledged, but everyone is free to participate as well.
3. *Interfaith gatherings with a shared order of service.* In such situations,
all present are participants, and there is an overarching theme.

These various kinds of service possess their own particular features. In the
first type, where adherents of one faith invite others to attend, they are not
seeking to make converts – rather there is a conscious recognition of the
integrity of other faith traditions. In such an environment, the proponents
of Pluralistic Judaism should feel comfortable – ideally, Jewish guests at
such a service would strive to enter into the religious experience itself.
Advocates of Pluralistic Judaism should not feel hesitant to recite prayers
or sing hymns whose truth-claims do not conform to the truth-claims of
Judaism. Given that God as He is in himself is unknowable, the different
formulations of faith in worship should be perceived as human constructions that strive to depict the nature of the Divine.

Similarly, in the second type of worship service, in which there is a serial
reading by representatives of other religions, Pluralistic Judaism would
welcome the opportunity to share the Jewish liturgical tradition. Those
who espouse this new philosophy of Judaism should not hesitate to join
in the liturgy from other traditions when appropriate. In accordance with
a pluralistic stance, such serial services are based on mutual respect and
allow each community an equal part in worship.

Turning to the third form of worship service, in which there is a joint
liturgy, Pluralistic Judaism would encourage Jews to pray with members
of other faiths. In such contexts, participants are often invited to worship
the One Eternal One – the ground of being in which all religious dogma
and ritual point at the Divine Mystery. This form of service is particularly
amenable to this new philosophy of Judaism in which God is viewed as
beyond human understanding. In services of this type the distinctiveness
of each religion is acknowledged – there is no attempt to replace the
regular liturgy of the individual faith-communities. Yet there is an implicit
assumption that, in worship, the followers of the world's religions stand
before the Ultimate, which they have described in different ways. The third
form of worship hence is consonant with the principles of Pluralistic
Judaism; it affirms other faiths while simultaneously recognizing the
limitations of human reason.

Pluralistic Judaism – as a new ideology for Judaism in the future – thus
not only provides a basis for reformulating the Jewish faith in the light of
contemporary theological reflection, it also serves as a framework for
interfaith encounter on the deepest level. If Judaism is to survive, what is

now required is the formulation of a modern conception of Judaism based on the recognition that the Jewish view of God is ultimately grounded in human experience and reflection. As such, Jews should no longer proclaim that their religious beliefs are absolute. Instead, these should be understood as no different in principle from those found in other religions. Such a theology of religious pluralism in which the Jewish faith is perceived simply as one religion among others demands an attitude of openness and receptivity. Unlike the various branches of contemporary Judaism, this interpretation of the Jewish heritage paves the way for a sympathetic appreciation of the riches of other religions, and calls for fruitful dialogue with the adherents of other faith-communities in a global context.

Here, then, is a new foundation for Jewish living in the future. Based on personal autonomy as a fundamental principle of Jewish life, this new philosophy of Judaism provides a basis for religious belief and practice as well as interfaith dialogue and encounter which conforms to the realities of everyday Jewish existence in Israel and the diaspora. In modern society, Jews across the religious spectrum determine for themselves which features of the Jewish tradition they find spiritually significant. Pluralistic Judaism, as portrayed in this book, acknowledges and celebrates this aspect of contemporary Jewish life. Respecting personal liberty and freedom, it offers the adherents of all the branches of Judaism a new perspective on religious faith in our troubled and troubling world.

Interreligious Exploration

Given the possibility for religious dialogue and encounter in the modern world, there are a number of central issues that Jews and adherents of other faiths could fruitfully explore together:

1. *Symbols.* Jews and members of other traditions could profitably explore the nature of religious symbols as long as neither the Jewish nor the non-Jewish partner adopts the standpoint that the symbols of his or her respective faith are superior.
2. *Worship.* In most of the religions of the world, worship is a response to the Divine, an acknowledgement of a reality independent of the worshipper. Assuming that neither the Jewish nor the non-Jewish participant in interfaith dialogue maintains that his or her conception of Ultimate Reality is uniquely true, it would be helpful to discuss the ways in

which various forms of worship provide some glimpse into the nature of Divine reality.

3. *Ritual.* Like worship, ritual plays a major role in the world's religions, and there are areas worthy of joint investigation as long as neither party adopts an attitude of religious superiority.

4. *Ethics.* Traditionally, Jews believe that God chose the Jewish nation to be his special people and gave them his law on Mount Sinai. The moral law is thus embodied in immutable, divine commandments. In other faiths, however, ethical values are perceived in a different light. The exploration of the foundations of alternative ethical systems could result in a deepening of ethical awareness.

5. *Society.* Religions are not only systems of belief and practice; they are also organizations that have a communal and social dimension. Given that neither the Jewish nor non-Jewish partner in dialogue assumes that their faith possesses a better organizational structure and a more positive attitude towards modern society, it would be of interest to examine the ways in which each religion understands itself in relation to the world.[8]

Appendix

Jews Worldwide

The number of Jews in the world before the outbreak of war in 1939 was about 17,000,000. Today, there are about 13,000,000 Jews worldwide in the following countries:

- Algeria (30): In 1962 there were around 120,000 Jews in Algeria, but after the struggle for independence, the Jews lost their possessions and left the country.
- Argentina (240,000): The early settlers in Argentina were Marranos. The present community grew through immigration, beginning in 1862 from Germany, the Balkans and North Africa. From Eastern Europe, immigrants began to arrive in 1889. Approximately 180,000 Jews live in Buenos Aires.
- Armenia (500): Jews have lived in Armenia for hundreds of years. Nowadays nearly all Armenian Jews live in Yerevan. Over 60 per cent of the population is over 60.
- Aruba (60): Jews from Curacao arrived in Aruba early in the nineteenth century; the present community dates from 1924.
- Australia (105,000): The earliest organization of Jews in Australia was in 1817. In public life Jews have played a distinguished part, many having risen to high office. The main Jewish communities are in Melbourne, Sydney, Perth, Brisbane, Adelaide, The Gold Coast, Queensland, Canberra and Hobart.
- Austria (12,000): After the 1848 Revolution, Jews gained equality and their economic and cultural importance grew. In 1941 Austria's Jewish population numbered 191,481, but it was destroyed by the Holocaust. Nearly all Austrian Jews now live in Vienna.
- Bahamas (200): The Freeport Hebrew Congregation consists of about 15 families.

- Barbados (55): A Jewish community was formed in Barbados by refugees from Recife in 1650. With the economic decline of the West Indies, the number of Jewish inhabitants decreased. In 1987 the Old Synagogue in Bridgetown reopened.
- Belarus (28,000): There are communities in Gommel, Grodno, Minsk, Orsha and Rechitsa.
- Belgium (30,000): Jews have lived in Belgium since Roman times. In 1830 the status of Jewry was formally recognized and the Constitution accorded them freedom of religion. Before the Second World War, the Jewish population was 80,000.
- Bermuda (125): The small community is drawn from a dozen countries.
- Bolivia (640): There have been Jews in Latin America for centuries, but they are comparative newcomers to Bolivia.
- Bosnia Herzegovina (1,100): There is a congregation in Sarajevo.
- Brazil (250,000): The Inquisition, revived in Brazil, increased the number of Marrano Jews. In 1624 Jews were granted full religious freedom. The majority of the population live in Sao Paulo State and Rio de Janeiro State.
- Bulgaria (6,500): Bulgarian Jewry dates from the second century CE. Before the Second World War there were about 50,000 Jews in Bulgaria. Today, most live in Sofia.
- Burma (25): About 25 Jews live in Rangoon.
- Canada (348,605): Jews were prohibited from living in Canada when it was a French possession. In the 1770s a Sephardic congregation was established in Montreal. In the nineteenth century, Jewish immigrants arrived in Canada in some numbers. At the end of the century, massive emigration from Eastern Europe began.
- Cayman Islands (60): There are about 60 Jewish residents in the three Cayman Islands.
- Chile (25,000): The majority of Chilean Jews live in the Santiago area.
- China (3,100): There is a community in Kaifeng that claims Jewish descent. Immigrants from Asia settled in China at the end of the nineteenth century; Russian and German refugees from the First and Second World War increased the population.
- Congo (100): Before the Congo attained independence from Belgian rule in 1960 there were about 2,500 Jews living there.
- Costa Rica (2,500): Most of the Jewish population live in San José.
- Croatia (2,500): There are nine Jewish communities in Croatia.
- Czech Republic (10,000): Jews lived in Bohemia in the eleventh

century and in Moravia as early as the ninth century. There were flourishing communities in the Middle Ages. In 1930 over 350,000 Jews lived in Czechoslovakia. The population was devastated by the Holocaust.

- Denmark (7,000): Jews lived in Denmark from the seventeenth century. Nearly all of their number today live in Copenhagen.
- Dominican Republic (150): The present community was formed before the Second World War.
- Ecuador (1,000): Most Ecuadorian Jews reside in Quito and Guayaquil.
- Egypt (240): The history of the community goes back to biblical times. About 150 Jews now live in Cairo and 50 in Alexandria.
- El Salvador (100): Most Jews here live in San Salvador.
- Fiji (20): About 12 Jewish families live in Suva.
- Finland (150): The settlement of Jews in Finland dates from about 1850. Most live in Helsinki.
- France (650,000): The first Jewish settlers arrived in France with the Greek founders of Marseilles in c. 500 BCE. After the destruction of the Second Temple, Jewish exiles established new communities. In 1791 French Jewry was emancipated. During the Second World War about 120,000 were deported or massacred. Since the war there has been an influx of Jews from Central and Eastern Europe as well as North Africa. Most live in Paris.
- Georgia (13,000): The Jews of Georgia are divided into two groups: native Georgian-speaking Jews and the Ashkenazi Jews who came to Georgia following its annexation by Russia at the beginning of the nineteenth century. The population declined due to emigration, mainly to Israel. Tbilisi has the largest Jewish population.
- Germany (108,000): A large Jewish community existed in Germany from Roman times. The Nazis destroyed the community, which numbered more than half a million before 1933.
- Gibraltar (600): The present Jewish community dates back to immigrants from North Africa shortly after the British annexation in 1704. During the siege of 1779 to 1783 the size of the population was reduced but increased subsequently.
- Greece (4,800): There have been Jewish communities in Greece since ancient times. Before 1939 there were over 70,000 Jews living in the country. Most of those remaining now live in Athens.
- Guatemala (1,500): Jews have lived here since 1898.
- Haiti (150): There has been a Jewish community here for the past 80 years.

- Honduras (150): There has been a Jewish community in Honduras for the past 50 years.
- Hungary (100,000): Jews have lived here since Roman times. Before the Second World War, the Jewish population was about 800,000. Some 600,000 perished in the Holocaust.
- India (5,600): The settlement of Jews in India goes back to the early centuries of the Christian era. Today there are four groups: (1) those who arrived in the last two centuries from Baghdad, Iran and Afghanistan; (2) Bene Israel, who believe their ancestors arrived in India after the destruction of the First Temple; (3) Cochin Jews, who have records going back to the fourth century CE; (4) European Jews who came within the last 50 years.
- Indonesia (16): The community is located in Surabaya.
- Iran (24,000): Jews have lived here since the sixth century BCE. From the beginning of the twentieth century the population has been under 70,000. Most live in Tehran, Shiraz, Isafan, Kerman and Kermanshah.
- ISRAEL (5,330,000): Palestine was administered until 14 May 1948 by Great Britain under a Mandate, which was approved by the League of Nations and incorporated the Balfour Declaration in its preamble. On 20 May 1947 the Assembly of the United Nations recommended the partition of Palestine into an Arab and Jewish state with an internationalized Jerusalem and district combined in an economic union. When the British surrendered the Mandate on 14 May 1948, Israel was declared as a state with a population of 655,000 under a provisional government, with Chaim Weizmann as President and David Ben-Gurion as Prime Minister. On 5 July 1950 the Law of Return was proclaimed, which conferred the right of every Jew to live in Israel.

  The Provisional Government of Israel was replaced by a permanent government after the election of the First Parliament (Knesset) in January 1949. Under Israeli law, elections must be universal, nationwide, secret and proportional. Elections are to be held every four years. The Knesset is elected by a form of proportional representation in which members are selected in proportion to the votes cast for each party. As a result of this system, no single party has yet been able to form a government on the basis of its own majority. Until the election of 1977 the dominant political force was a coalition of the Left; this formed governments with the help of various smaller parties, usually those of a religious nature. In the elections of 1977 and 1981 an alliance of the Right was able to form an administration with the help of religious parties.

Within recent years there has been a polarization of attitudes among sections of Israeli society; this was reflected by the proliferation of small parties which contested the 1984 election. The 1984 election produced an inconclusive result, with only three seats separating the two big party blocs that formed Israel's second national unity government. The office of Prime Minister was held in rotation. The 1988 election was also inclusive and was followed by another coalition government. The national unity government broke up in March 1990 when Likud declined to support a US Plan to promote peace talks. The elections of 1992 produced a Labour coalition led by Yitzhak Rabin. This outcome was due in part to the influx of settlers from Eastern Europe as well as to political and economic pressures. The Knesset elections of 1996 were the first in which there was direct voting for Prime Minister. Following the resignation of Mr Barak in 2001, Ariel Sharon was elected Prime Minister. Although political power rests constitutionally in the Knesset, the President of Israel can in certain circumstances exercise a degree of power. The President is elected for a five-year period, renewable only once.

The major political parties are:

Israel Labour Party: Established by the merger of Mapai, Achdut Avoda and Rafi, its programme is 'to attain national, social and pioneering aims, in the spirit of the Jewish people, the vision of socialist Zionism and the values of the Labour movement'.

Kadima: A new party that defines itself as a broad popular movement that works to ensure the future of Israel as a Jewish democratic state. The party was formed by Ariel Sharon in November 2005 following the Israeli withdrawal from Gaza. It split from the Likud alliance.

Likud: A Conservative political party dedicated to the principles of free-market economy and the attainment of peace with security while preserving Israel's national interests.

Meretz-Yachad: This party was formed in 1992 by a merger of Ratz, Mapam, and the Shinui Party. It disbanded in 2003 and joined the Shahar Party, which renamed itself Yachad, but the original name re-emerged in 1005. It is a Zionist Green left-wing social democratic party.

Gil: A party committed to supporting pensioners.

National Religious Party: Created through the merger of Mizrachi and Hapoel Hamizrachi in 1956, this party's motto is: 'The People of Israel in the Land of Israel, according to the Torah of Israel'.

Shinui: A reformist and liberal party.

Agudat Israel: Founded in 1912 in Poland, its principle is that only the Torah unites the Jewish people.

Shas: The Shas party was formed under the leadership of Rabbi Ovadia Yosef, a former Israeli Chief Rabbi.

Yisrael Beytenu: A right-wing party formed in 1997 to create a platform for Russian immigrants who support a hard line in negotiations with the Palestinian authority.

- Italy (34,500): The Jewish community goes back to very early times, and during the Middle Ages and the Renaissance there were newcomers from Spain and Germany respectively. During the period 1943–5, nearly 12,000 Jews were murdered or banished. Most remaining Jews live in Rome, Milan and Turin.
- Jamaica (350): The Jewish settlement in Jamaica goes back before the British occupation in 1655. During the eighteenth century there was an influx of Ashkenazi Jews from England.
- Japan (2,000): The first Japanese Jewish community dates back to 1860. Jews were among the early foreign settlers. In 1940 about 5,000 immigrants arrived from Germany and Poland. Most Jews today live in Tokyo.
- Kazakhstan (7,000): The Jews here are predominately Russian-speaking Ashkenazim. Many arrived in the 1940s. Almaty is the main Jewish centre.
- Kenya (100 families): A Jewish settlement in East Africa dates from 1903. Most who live here are Israelis, together with those who are in the diplomatic services.
- Kyrgyzstan (1,500): Most Jews here live in Frunze.
- Latvia (10,800): Most Latvian Jews live in Riga and speak Russian.
- Lebanon (100): In the civil war that broke out in 1975, most of the 2,000 Jews left the country.
- Libya (50): When Libya became independent in 1951, there was a mass emigration of about 37,000 Jews to Israel.
- Lithuania (11,000): Most Lithuanian Jews live in Vilnius and Kaunas.
- Luxembourg (1,000): The majority of Jews here live in Luxembourg City.
- Malta (50): There have been Jews in Malta since pre-Roman times. The Maltese Jewish community now owns its own property, after a gap of 500 years.
- Mexico (40,000): The Jewish population in Mexico dates back to the Spanish conquest. It was not until the final years of the

nineteenth century and the beginning of the twentieth that a mass immigration of Jews from the Balkanic countries and Eastern Europe took place. The majority of Jews live in Mexico City.

- Morocco (5,000): The Jews of Morocco date back to before it became a Roman province. Expulsion from Spain and Portugal brought many Jews to Morocco. Before the establishment of the kingdom of Morocco in 1956 many Jews emigrated to Israel, France, Spain and Canada.
- The Netherlands (25,000): From the sixteenth century onwards the Jews of the provinces of Holland prospered. Since 1792 they have had the same constitutional and civil rights as other citizens. In 1940 there were about 140,000 Jews in the country. Most live in Amsterdam.
- Netherlands Antilles (350): A Sephardi settlement was established here in 1652. About 350 Jews live in Curacao.
- New Caledonia (120): About 120 Jews live on this French possession in the Pacific.
- New Zealand (8,000): The settlement of Jews here dates from the establishment of British sovereignty in 1840. Jews have occupied important positions in New Zealand, including that of Administrator, Prime Minister, and Chief Justice.
- Pakistan (2 Jewish families): Two Jewish families live in Karachi.
- Panama (9,250): The Jewish community in Panama has been in existence for nearly 150 years. Most live in Panama City.
- Paraguay (900): The community here has been in existence since 1912.
- Peru (3,000): Marranos were prominent in the early development of the country. Many Jews were martyred during the time of the Inquisition. Most live in Lima.
- Philippines (250): Jews fled to the Philippines during the Spanish colonial era, but postwar emigration has reduced the population to around 250.
- Poland (6,000): Jews first settled in Poland in the twelfth century. Jewish learning flourished in the country from the sixteenth century. In 1939 there were about 3,500,000 Jews in Poland. Until 1968 there were about 50,000 Jews in the country; large-scale emigration followed the anti-Jewish policy pursued under the guise of anti-Zionism.
- Portugal (1,000): Between the twelfth and fifteenth centuries Jews in Portugal lived in relative peace. However, the Expulsion Edict of 1496 was followed by forced conversions and the establishment of the Inquisition. For three centuries, up to the 1800s, there were officially

no Jews in Portugal. Nonetheless, a number of Marrano groups survived. At the beginning of the nineteenth century a large number of Jews from Gibraltar and Morocco settled in Lisbon, Faro and the Azores Islands. Today, there are three Jewish communities in Portugal.

- Puerto Rico (1,500): Jews were officially prohibited from settling in Puerto Rico for much of its history, but the island is now home to one of the largest Jewish communities in the Caribbean.
- Romania (10,000): Jews have lived in the territory that now forms Romania since Roman times. Today, most live in Bucharest.
- Russia (440,000): Before the First World War, Russian Jewry comprised the largest Jewish community in the world despite persecution under the policy of the tsars. The subsequent Soviet regime virtually destroyed the religious life and organization of the Jewish community. According to the 1989 census, the Jewish population was nearly 1,500,000, but mass emigration reduced that number.
- Serbia (3,500): Jews have lived in this territory since Roman times. In 1941 there were about 34,000 Jews living in the country.
- Singapore (240): The Jewish community of Singapore dates from about 1840.
- Slovakia (6,000): The Jews of Slovakia go back to the thirteenth century.
- South Africa (75,000): The Jewish community began as an organized body in 1841 in Cape Town. Jews have had connections with the Cape of Good Hope from the earliest days of South African history.
- South Korea (25 families): Most of the 25 Jewish families here live in Seoul.
- Spain (25,000): Jews settled in Spain in Roman times. Persecution by the Church culminated in the Inquisition and expulsion of 1492. Most Jews live in Barcelona, Madrid and Malaga.
- Suriname (300): Suriname is one of the oldest Jewish settlements in the Western hemisphere. The Sephardi congregation was established in 1661.
- Sweden (18,000): The first Jews in Sweden were granted the right to live there in 1774. Later, Jews were admitted to Stockholm, Gothenburg and Norrköping.
- Switzerland (17,600): Jews were expelled from Switzerland in the fifteenth century and it was not until the seventeenth that they were allowed to settle in the country. In 1856 immigration increased with an influx of Jews from Southern Germany, Alsace and Eastern Europe.

- Syria (1,500): Jews reside in Damascus, Aleppo and Kamishli.
- Tahiti (130): The majority of Jews here live on the Pacific Island of Tahiti.
- Taiwan (180): Most Taiwanese Jews live in Taipei.
- Tajikistan (1,000): The Jews of Tajikistan are divided into two groups: Bukharan Jews and later arrivals of Ashkenazi origin. The Bukharan Jews speak Bukhori or Judeo-Tajik.
- Tunisia (3,000): The history of the Jewish community here dates from antiquity. In 1881 Jews obtained equal rights with Muslims. The population fell from nearly 100,000 in 1950 to 25,000 in June 1967, and later to a much smaller number.
- Turkey (25,000): During the Spanish Inquisition, the Ottoman Empire was one of the principal lands of refuge for Jews. With the proclamation of the Turkish Republic, Jews gained citizenship rights.
- Turkmenistan (1,000): In 1989 about 2,500 Jews lived here.
- Ukraine (300,000): Various Jewish organizations are based in Kiev.
- United States of America (5,280,000): Although there were individual Jewish settlers before 1654 in the territory that is now the United States, it was not until then that Jewish immigrants arrived in a group at New Amsterdam (renamed New York in 1664). Twenty-three of these came from Brazil by way of Cuba and Jamaica. Through successive waves of immigration resulting from persecution in Russia, Poland, Romania, Germany and other countries, the Jewish population underwent massive increases. Today, the largest segment of American Jewry (1,720,000) live in the New York metropolitan area.
- Uruguay (25,000): Jewish immigration to Uruguay began in the early twentieth century. About 10,000 Jews fled there with Hitler's rise to power. Large numbers emigrated there after the war. In the 1940s about 50,000 Jews lived in the country. Most live in Montevideo.
- Uzbekistan (35,000): Most Jews here live in Tashkent, Samarkand and Bukhara.
- Venezuela (20,000): The first Jewish community in Venezuela was established by Sephardi Jews early in the nineteenth century. Most live in Caracas.
- Virgin Islands (350): Jews have lived here since the eighteenth century and have played an important role in the country.[1]

Notes

Introduction

1   Mishnah, 'Sayings of the Fathers', l:2.
2   Talmud, 'Shabbath', XLIX.
3   'Pact of Omar', in Jacob Rader Marcus (ed), *The Jew in the Medieval World*, Athenaeum, 1977, pp. 13–14.
4   Saadiah Gaon, 'The Refutation of Anan', in Dan and Lavinia Cohn-Sherbok, *A Short Reader in Judaism*, Oneworld, 1977, pp. 81–2.
5   In Leon Poliakov, *History of Anti-Semitism*, Littman Library, Vol. 1, 1974, p. 59.
6   'Edict of Expulsion', in Cohn-Sherbok, *A Short Reader in Judaism*, p. 88.
7   Hayyim Vital, *Etz Hayyim*, in Dan Cohn-Sherbok, *Jewish Mysticism: An Anthology*, Oneworld, 1995.
8   Paul Rycaut, *History of the Turkish Empire*, in Cohn-Sherbok, *A Short Reader in Judaism*, pp. 110–11.
9   Martin Luther, 'Against the Jews and Their Lies', in Dan Cohn-Sherbok, *The Crucified Jew*, HarperCollins, 1992, pp. 72–3.
10   Aaron of Apt, 'Kether Shem Tov', in Cohn-Sherbok, *A Short Reader in Judaism*, p. 117.
11   Moses Mendelssohn, *Jerusalem*, in Cohn-Sherbok, *A Short Reader in Judaism*, p. 130.

Chapter 1

1   Singer's Prayer Book, p. 17.
2   Martin Buber, *Tales of the Hasidim*, Vol. I, p. 212.
3   *Exodus Rabbah*, Yitro, 28:4.
4   *Commentary to the Mishnah*, Sanhedrin X, I.
5   *Mahzor for Rosh Hashanah and Yom Kippur*, The Rabbinic Assembly, 2000, pp. 377–81.
6   Joseph Hertz, *Daily Prayer Book*, Bloch, 1948, p. 409.
7   Hertz, *Daily Prayer Book*, p. 119.
8   Hertz, *Daily Prayer Book*, p. 119.
9   *Numbers Rabbah*, Naso, 11:2.
10   Hertz, *Daily Prayer Book*, pp. 357–9.
11   *Mahzor for Rosh Hashanah and Yom Kippur*, pp. 407–8.
12   *Siddur Sim Shalom*, Rabbinic Assembly, 1985, p. 243.
13   Hayim Goldin, *Hamadrich*, Hebrew Publishing Company, 1956, p. 54.
14   *Hamadrich*, pp. 15–17.
15   www.jwn.org.uk/limmud011.htm.

Chapter 2

1   'Edict of Joseph II', in Cohn-Sherbok, *A Short Reader in Judaism*, p. 128.
2   'Edict of the Russian Church, 1807', in Cohn-Sherbok, *A Short Reader in Judaism*, p. 129.
3   Nicholas I, 'Delineation of the Pale of Settlement', in Paul Mendes-Flohr and Jehuda Reinharz (eds), *The Jewish in the Modern World*, Oxford University Press, 1995, p. 379.
4   'Constitution of the Hamburg Temple', in Cohn-Sherbok, *A Short Reader in Judaism*, p. 132.
5   Samson Raphael Hirsch, 'Religion Allied to Progress', in Mendes-Flohr and Reinharz (eds), *The Jew in the Medieval World*, p. 132.
6   'Pittsburgh Platform', in Cohn-Sherbok, *A Short Reader in Judaism*, pp. 135–6.
7   Wilhelm Marr, 'The Victory of Judaism over Germandom', in Mendes-Flohr and Reinharz (eds), *The Jew in the Modern World*, pp. 331–2.
8   Houston Stewart Chamberlain, 'The Foundations of the Nineteenth Century', in Mendes-Flohr and Reinharz (eds), *The Jew in the Modern World*, pp. 358–9.

9   Leon Pinsker, 'Autoemancipation', in Arthur Hertzberg, *The Zionist Idea: A Historical Analysis and Reader*, Athenaeum, 1959, p. 188.

10   Theodor Herzl, 'A Solution to the Jewish Question', in Mendes-Flohr and Reinharz (eds), *The Jew in the Modern World*, pp. 553–4.

11   'Proclamation of the State of Israel', in Mendes-Flohr and Reinharz (eds), *The Jew in the Modern World*, p. 629.

Chapter 3

1   Adolph Hitler, 'Mein Kampf', in Cohn-Sherbok, *A Short Reader in Judaism*, p. 154.

2   Stanislav Rozyck, 'Description of the Warsaw Ghetto', in Dan Cohn-Sherbok, *Understanding the Holocaust*, Continuum, 1995, pp. 127–8.

3   Rudolf Reder, 'Belzec', in Cohn-Sherbok, *Understanding the Holocaust*, p. 159.

4   Austin J. App, 'The Six Million Swindle', in Cohn-Sherbok, *Understanding the Holocaust*, pp. 257–8.

5   Deborah Lipstadt, *Denying the Holocaust: The Growing Assault on Truth and Memory*, Plume, 1993, pp. 216–17.

6   Richard Rubenstein, *After Auschwitz*, Indianapolis, 1966, p. 153.

7   David Ariel, *What Do Jews Believe?*, Rider, 1996, p. 105.

8   Eliezer Berkovits, *Faith after the Holocaust*, KTAV, 1973, pp. 63–4.

9   Emil Fackenheim, 'Jewish Faith and the Holocaust' in Michael Morgan (ed), *The Jewish Thought of Emil Fackenheim*, Wayne State University Press, 1987, p. 176.

10   'The Peel Commission', in Cohn-Sherbok, *A Short Reader in Judaism*, p. 159.

11   David Ben-Gurion, Israel: 'The Years of Challenge', in Cohn-Sherbok, *A Short Reader in Judaism*, pp. 160–1.

12   'Law Enacted by the Knesset, 1960', in Cohn-Sherbok, *A Short Reader in Judaism*, p. 161.

13   www.palestinefacts.org/Sharon-speech_8apr02.php.

14   Dan Cohn-Sherbok and Dawoud El-Alami, *The Palestine Israeli Conflict*, Oneworld, 2008, pp. 116–17.

15   BBC News report, 19 March 2009, available at http://news.bbc.co.uk/1/hi/7952603.stm.

Chapter 4

1   'The Community Patriarch', in Dan and Lavinia Cohn-Sherbok, *The American Jew*, HarperCollins, pp. 180–1.

2   'The University Professor of Judaica', in Cohn-Sherbok, *The American Jew*, pp. 97–100.

3   'Aaron of Apt, Kether Shem Tov', in Cohn-Sherbok, *A Short Reader in Judaism*, p. 117.

4   Zecharias Frankel, 'On Changes in Judaism', in Mendes-Flohr and Reinharz (ed), *The Jew in the Modern World*, pp. 194–5.

5   'The Reconstructionist Leader', in Cohn-Sherbok, *The American Jew*, p. 51.

6   Abraham Geiger, 'Jewish Scholarship and Religious Belief', in Mendes-Flohr and Reinharz (eds), *The Jew in the Modern World*, p. 233.

7   *Guide to Humanistic Judaism*, Society of Humanistic Judaism, p. 70.

8   www.thaivisa.com/forum/Spiritual-Blend-Jubus-t75925.html.

9   David Rausch, *Messianic Judaism: Its History, Theology and Polity*, Edwin Mellen, 1982, p. 120.

10 En.wikipedia.org/wiki/Jewish-Renewal.

11 Philip Berg, 'Kabbalah for the Layman', in Cohn-Sherbok, *Kabbalah and Jewish Mysticism: An Anthology*, p. 155.

12 In Cohn-Sherbok, *The American Jew*, pp. 258–9.

13 www.aish.com/h/15sh/i/48967316.html.

14 www.glbtjews.org/article.php37id-article=122.

Chapter 5

1   'The Restauranteur', in Cohn-Sherbok, *The American Jew*, p. 246.

2   Bernard Maza, *With Fury Poured Out*, KTAV, 1986, pp. 124–7.

3   Ignaz Maybaum, *The Face of God after Auschwitz*, Polak and Van Gennep, 1965, pp. 66–7.

4   Mordecai Kaplan, *Judaism as a Civilization*, Schocken, 1967, pp. 317–18.

5   Sigmund Freud, *The Future of an Illusion*, Hogarth Press, 1981, pp. 16–17.

6   'Code of Hammurabi', in A. C. Bouquet, *Sacred Books of the World*, Penguin, 1959, pp. 44–5.

7   'Gilgamesh Epic', in Bouquet, *Sacred Books of the World*, p. 51.

8   Mordecai Kaplan, 'The Meaning of God for the Contemporary Jew', in A. Jospe (ed), *Tradition and Contemporary Experience*, Schocken, 1970, pp. 70–3.
9   *Guide to Humanistic Judaism*, Society for Humanistic Judaism, 1993, pp. 5–6.
10   Louis Jacobs, *Principles of the Jewish Faith*, London, 1964, pp. 388–9.
11   'Pittsburgh Platform', in Cohn-Sherbok, *Modern Judaism*, Macmillan, 1996, p. 83.
12   Solomon Freehof, *Reform Responsa*, CCAR, 1960, pp. 22–3.
13   www.myjewishlearning.com/history/Modern-History/1980–2000/ American-Jewish-Community/Patrilineal Descent.shtml.
14   www.answers.com/topic/law-of-return.
15   Jonathan Sacks, *One People? Tradition and Modernity and Jewish Unity*, London, 1993, p. 219.

Chapter 6

1   *Siddar Avodat Israel*, Sinai Publishing, 1967, p. 9.
2   In Cohn-Sherbok, *Jewish Mysticism: An Anthology*, p. 80.
3   'Zohar', in Cohn-Sherbok, *The Jewish Faith*, SPCK, 1993, p. 172.
4   Dan Cohn-Sherbok, *Judaism: History, Belief and Practice*, Routledge, 2003, p. 545.
5   John Hick, *Philosophy of Religion*, Prentice Hall, 1973, p. 103.
6   Ben Zion Bokser, *Jewish Law: A Conservative Approach*, Burning Book Press, 1964, pp. 12–13.
7   Wilfred Cantwell Smith, *The Faith of Other Men*, New York, 1962, p. 123.
8   In Dan Cohn-Sherbok, *The Future of Judaism*, London, pp. 206–8.

Appendix

1   See *Jewish Year Book*, ed. Stephen W. Massil, London: Valentine Mitchell, 2009.

Select Readings

Ariel, David (1996), *What Do Jews Believe? The Jewish Faith Examined*, London: Rider.

Avineri, Shlomo (1981), *The Making of Modern Zionism: Intellectual Origins of the Jewish State*, New York: Basic Books.

Ben-Sasson, Hayim (1985), *The History of the Jewish People*, Cambridge, MA: Harvard University Press.

Borowitz, Eugene (1983), *Choices in Modern Jewish Thought*, New York: Behrman House.

Donin, Hayim Halevy (1991), *To Pray as a Jew: A Guide to the Prayer Book and the Synagogue Service*, New York: Basic Books.

Gilbert, Martin (1998), *Israel: A History*, New York: William Morrow and Co.

Gilbert, Martin (1987), *The Holocaust*, New York: HarperCollins.

Gillman, Neil (1992), Sacred Fragments: *Reconverting Theology for the Modern Jew*, New York: Jewish Publication Society.

Goldberg, Michael (1995), *Why Should Jews Survive?*, Oxford and New York: Oxford University Press.

Greenberg, Irving (1980), *On the Third Era in Jewish History*, New York: National Jewish Resource Centre.

Jacobs, Louis (1964), *Principles of the Jewish Faith*, London: Vallentine Mitchell.

Jacobs, Louis (1973), *A Jewish Theology*, New York: Behrman House.

Jacobs, Steven (1994), *Rethinking Jewish Faith*, New York: State University of New York Press.

Lange, Nicholas De (1986), *Judaism*, Oxford: Oxford University Press.

Lerner, Michael (1995), *Jewish Renewal: Path to Healing and Transformation*, San Francisco, Harper Perennial.

Marmur, Dov (1982), *Beyond Survival*, London: Darton, Longman and Todd.

Massil, Stephen W. (ed.) (2009), *Jewish Year Book*, London: Valentine Mitchell.

Mendes-Flohr, Paul R. and Reinharz, Jehuda (eds) (1995), *The Jew in the Modern World: A Documentary History*, New York: Oxford University Press.

Meyer, Michael A. (1990), *Response to Modernity: A History of the Reform Movement in Judaism*, New York: Oxford University Press.

Neusner, Jacob (1993), *Classical Judaism: Learning*, Essen and New York: Peter Lang.

Neusner, Jacob (2002), *Rabbinic Judaism: The Theological System*, Leiden, Brill and New York: Prometheus Books.

Plaskow, Judith (1990), *Again at Sinai: Judaism from a Feminist Perspective*, San Francisco: HarperCollins.

Potok, Chaim (1987), *Wanderings: Chaim Potok's History of the Jews*, New York: Fawcett Books.

Raphael, M. L. (1988), *Profiles in American Judaism*, New York: HarperCollins.

Rubenstein, Richard and Roth, John (1987), *Approaches to Auschwitz*, London: SCM.

Rubenstein, W. D. (1995), *The History of the Jews in the English-Speaking World*, London: Palgrave Macmillan.

Sachar, Howard Morley (1990), *The Course of Modern Jewish History*, New York: Vintage.

Schauss, Hayyim (1996), *The Jewish Festivals: A Guide to their History and Observance*, Berlin and New York: Schocken.

Seltzer, Robert (1980), *Jewish People, Jewish Thought*, New York: Macmillan.

Solomon, Norman (1991), *Judaism and World Religion*, London: Macmillan.

Sonsino, Rifat and Syme, Daniel (1990), *What Happens After I Die: Jewish Views of Life after Death*, New York: UAHC Press.

Trepp, Leo (1973), *A History of the Jewish Experience: Eternal Faith, Eternal People*, New York: Behrman House.

Unterman, Alan (1996), *Jews: Their Religious Beliefs and Practices*, Portland, OR: Sussex Academic Press.

Waskow, Arthur (1986), *Seasons of Our Joy: Handbook of Jewish Festivals*, Riverside, NJ: Simon & Schuster.

Webber, Jonathan (ed.) (1994), *Jewish Identities in the New Europe*, London: Littman Library.

Wyschograd, Michael (1996), *The Body of Faith: God and the People of Israel*, Northvale, NJ: Jason Aronson.

Index

1171371R0

Printed in Great Britain by
Amazon.co.uk, Ltd.,
Marston Gate.